REPROGRAMMING

THE

OVERWEIGHT MIND®

7 STEPS TO TAKING CONTROL OF YOUR SUBCONSCIOUS

ILLUMINE STUDIOS

Disclaimer Notice:

Mention of specific companies, organizations, or authorities does not imply an endorsement by the publisher nor does mention of specific companies, organizations, or authorities imply that they endorse this book.

Internet addresses given in this book were accurate at the time it went to press.

The author and publisher shall have neither liability nor responsibility to any person or entity with respect to any loss or damage caused, or alleged to be caused, directly or indirectly by the information contained in this book.

If you do not wish to be bound by the above, you may return the book to the publisher for a full refund.

The Overweight Mind is a registered trademark of Burris MIND/FITNESS.

All Rights Reserved.

Printed in the United States of America

Book Cover Design by Dylan Burris
Editor - Shirley Burris
Published by Illumine Studios
For more about this author go to www.KellyBurris.com

Library of Congress Cataloging-in-Publication Data

Burris, Kelly
        Reprogramming the overweight mind :
7 steps to taking control of your subconscious / Kelly Burris
        p. cm
LCCN 2004093061
ISBN 0-9644241-2-6

        1. Weight loss 2. Weight Loss — Psychological Aspects
3. Obesity — Psychological Aspects 4. Eating Disorders I Title

RM222.2.B87 2004   6132'5

QB133-2086

ACKNOWLEDGMENTS

I began the quest of getting control of the human machine in the late sixties and there are so many people responsible for this end result that it would take another book to thank them all. Because of this I will have to start at the turning point and that was with a chance meeting of a childhood hero.

I was out to dinner just after moving to Los Angeles in the early 1980s with a friend who worked a soap called *Days of Our Lives*. A woman who happened to watch the soap recognized the woman I was with and introduced herself and her father-in-law Fayard Nicholas of the Nicholas Brothers. I had been involved in dance and theatre from the age of four and the Nicholas Brothers were one of those bigger than life figures. Fayard invited us over to watch some of the old time films, and after we finished watching film from the old Cotton Club, Fayard explained to me that he and his brother were not allowed to go to the club other than as performers. I was thinking to myself how could someone do this to this great man. I became absolutely enraged while the smile on Fayard's face never left him. Fayard expressed nothing but love for his life, the opportunities that he had. In the midst of my anger at the Cotton Club story, I asked myself, "How does he do that? How can he express nothing but love even after being treated so poorly!?"

It was this question that would be the turning point for the development of this book and what is now the most powerful program process for behavior change.

My mother was an RN and a tremendous healer. I knew of course that love was the supreme power as exampled by her but the question was how to maintain it.

Barry Brenner MD PhD was the next big step in the development of this program process. He gave me access to a large number of physicians and psychologists who were instrumental in the development.

Bob Levin MA was a dedicated psychologist who felt that you should go beyond your training. He was instrumental in the early developmental stages of the program.

Kay Pitzenberger MA was the psychologist who not only helped in the compiling of the Emotional Checklist, she was also the one who helped me introduce MIND/FITNESS to her eating disorder patients in 1990 with tremendous success. Kay is a dedicated psychologist who fought to make a difference. She recommended to the corporation that she was working for, that MIND/FITNESS be integrated into their eating disorder program.

RJ Koval MD BSP was responsible for the first official clinical studies of MIND/FITNESS in 1992. He also recommended the program process to corporate executives at a large medical weight loss center.

Mike Kolpack MA was responsible for helping me break down the program to more digestible parts.

The foundation of my existence is my family and if not for the moral and financial support of my brothers Mike and Mark, this book would not have been possible.

Anyone with children knows that they are everything. My son Dylan has been the single biggest cause for change plus the development and refinement of the **MIND/FITNESS Program**.

CONTENTS

PART ONE:
MIND/FITNESS

The Weight Loss Industry And Eating Disorders

PART TWO:

7 Steps to Taking Control of Your Subconscious

PART THREE:

Food & Fitness Recommendations

APPENDICES

APPENDIX A

Appendix B

PART ONE

Burris MIND/FITNESS
The Weight Loss Industry
And Eating Disorders

I

WHAT DETERMINES YOUR EMOTIONAL STATE AND EATING BEHAVIOR

A brief history of MIND/FITNESS

By the age of 16 I was actively looking for an answer to how to take control of erratic out-of-control behaviors that included binge eating. By age 19 I had researched all of the major religions, I had studied the inner workings of Frederick Nietzsche and I had explored the work, research and theories of Gestalt, Pavlov and Freud. None of this led to any sort of answer except that blaming my life on someone or something else did not fix the problem. I had to own my current mental state if there was to be any chance of fixing myself.

My only true savior at the time was a rational thinking woman whom I married at 21. This of course did not stop the mania, depression or compulsive behavior, in particular my preferred primary drug…food. I am not going to go into the details of my compulsions because this book is not about that. It is about fixing the problem.

Having a child was the breaking point for me. Everyone has a breaking point and this was mine. I simply could not take the thought of passing along what I considered to be obscene behaviors to my child. I knew I was on a sinking ship and was absolutely not going to take my son or my wife down with me. There was no question at that point that I had to fix the machine. By age 28 I was divorced and still on a downward slide. There were so many times when I thought it could not get worse and it would. I continued my quest to fix the self and increased the attacks on the body to try and change the mind.

Like many people with a dance and theatrical background, I became a fitness and aerobics instructor in the late 70s. In 1982 I moved to Los Angeles and in 1984 I established a partnership with a brilliant MD PhD.

Continuing to attack the body to try and change the mind

I finally felt as though I was going to get supreme control via a more sophisticated means of data collection and implementation. This of course was not to be the case.

Dr. Brenner and I developed a comprehensive computer-assisted diet/exercise program that educated the patient on every aspect of their physiology. My specialty was the musculoskeletal system. The testing that I put the patient through included range of motion, gait assessment, musculoskeletal alignment, body fat analysis and of course strength testing to determine where their lifting program should start. We would also analyze food intake via a software program that broke down over 10,000 foods into fats, carbohydrates, vitamins, minerals and of course calories.

I could also monitor their fitness schedule with a heart rate watch that used a strap around the chest. The watch would memorize the workout which could be downloaded into a computer every week. If the patient was not reaching their goal weight, I could simply do the math and give the patient the option to cut calories or increase their fitness program.

The doctor's specialty was the cardiopulmonary system. He started with an extensive physical exam that included a stress test, oxygen uptake, full blood panel and any additional tests that may be needed as a result of a red flag. All data collection was logged into the computer which generated the most comprehensive musculoskeletal and cardiopulmonary evaluation available, all organized in a computer-generated document that was given to the patient. Once this was completed it would allow a patient to establish and maintain the perfect diet and exercise program for the rest of his or her life. The success rate for creating a permanent behavioral change however remained the same.

We had developed a system that was on par, if not more advanced, than what was used to test the athletes for the 1984 Olympics and professional athletes were the only people it worked for. This was the last time I would attack the body to try and change the mind. I suppose I needed to push it as far as it could go before the realization of having the best technology and the best minds telling you what to do was simply not going to work.

Some people consider the definition of insanity is to continue doing something that does not work. If you accept this definition then the community of psychology and entire weight loss industry is completely insane. We are still being sold on the idea that being obese is the result of some outside force that can be fixed by some product completely unrelated to the problem. I am here to tell you that all of this is about to change.

A new mindset

Having researched all of the most renowned psychologists, I felt as though I was completing a large circle but my only choice was to go back into the processes of the mind because I had done everything else. One of the many virtues of the relationship with Dr. Brenner is that I had access to an incredible array of physicians and psychologists. In a state of complete frustration, I decided to get to the core of the problem and concentrated my efforts on the behavioral aspects of diet and exercise in conjunction with several psychologists. After going through a couple of libraries of information over a period of two years, the result was a radical new approach to creating behavior change, not just in regard to diet and exercise but with all behaviors that were determined not beneficial.

The focus of the development of the program was not why people did what they did but on how a change could be made in the subconscious programming of each person. A behavior was looked upon as something that was learned and by using the same principles it took to learn the behavior, a program was formed to guide individuals through the process of how to unlearn a behavior that did not work and replace it with one that works better. After extensive testing the program found its final form in 1989 and an additional one-hundred overweight people used the program with dramatic results.

This led me to put the program to the ultimate test a year later. I introduced the program into a psychiatric care facility that specialized in eating disorders. The initial results were very positive and the following is a response from the psychologist who was also the Program Director of the women's program one and a half years later. *"Responses were very positive and in patient contact a year later, patients revealed positive on-going effects and affirmations of beginning life changes as a result of classes attended. I highly recommend this program to all."*

Kay Pitzenberger, M.A. Program
Director, Women's Program

In 1992 I performed several more clinical studies with obese patients in Dallas Texas at the offices of R.J. Koval MD, BSP. Before doing so the program met with some rigid scrutiny from the Director of Program Support at Jason Pharmaceuticals the parent company of Medifast. After evaluating the program this was the comment from the Director of Program Support in regard to other forms of treatment for obesity and MIND/FITNESS. *"The mind is dulled, befuddled, and numbed by a host of medications while the root of the problem remains in active force. Your program frees the soul to say, I can change my mind about myself. I can be in control. It goes beyond the power of positive thinking because it gives the steps, not just the pep talk."*

Janna Thornton
Director of Program Support

The Dallas studies brought many things to light. With depression as the key focus and a 54% improvement of depression symptoms over a five-day period, other important issues arose. According to another study published by *The Journal of Nutrition Education*, self-confidence was the single most important factor for people to accomplish their weight loss goals. In the five-day study group self-confidence rose 100%.

Needless to say the bariatric physician that administered the studies was very impressed and had this to say after closely evaluating the results of the clinical studies. *"Over the past 27 years of my medical practice, I've always felt that there was something missing from the weight loss equation. I've slowly come to realize that all diets, including Medifast are externally imposed. To be truly effective, long term, the weight loss has to originate internally. Success has to come from within, not from without. Maybe that is why so many people regain their weight—very few have been practicing the techniques to effectively control their actions! The Burris Program is the first treatment that directly attacks this problem!"*

There were many positive comments from the Dallas study but one in particular got my attention because of what was to follow. *"I have tried many weight-loss programs and over two years of professional counseling and have literally spent 1000s of dollars to no avail. In one short week Mr. Burris gave me control over my life. Notice I said life not just my eating. His program showed me how I could regain control over all compulsive activity."*

Lisa Watford
School Teacher

I had many like this before but it was a letter from Lisa that was and is today the most impressive because of the use of MIND/ FITNESS to allow children to take control of there own programming.
Dear Mr. Burris,

Discipline is the most difficult issue educators and students face in today's classroom. An enriching learning environment can not take place without it. If a child does not feel secure within the confines of the classroom then long term learning will not take place.

As an educator, I use the Burris program to teach fifth grade students how to deal with life and its complexities. Our classroom has gone from a virtual minefield of aggressive behavior, peppered with verbal confrontations, into a safe haven from which all to pass, parent and teachers included.

I have been told there is something very different about the way my students treat and respect each other, themselves, and authority. Students learn their own personal tools to change any negative behavior. Issues are confronted and turned into positive questioning skills. We use the Burris questions from the Heart of MIND/FITNESS as our daily Journal topics. If someone is talking negatively about them self or anyone else we stop and deal with how to turn that negative statement into a positive question. For example, one of my students kept saying she was a "klutz," while her mother concurred. The students came up with one simple question. "What steps can I take to become more graceful?" The child is a different person. The lack of physical coordination is gone. She is actually more graceful and confident than the rest of my students. The questioning techniques of the Burris program are phenomenal and the results are immediate. Students learn they don't have any control over an adult's behavior, but they do have control over how they respond to the adults. When children are allowed to take control of their behavior, they react appropriately; not because they want to please the teacher, but because they have internalized the correct decisions and choose to act positively. We use positive questions for students with conduct marks. For example, a student who has trouble getting along with his peers will have to write the same question 25 times. "What changes do I need to make in order to get along well with my peers?" The Burris program teaches students life skills to find the best solutions. Grades and conduct have improved beyond even what I could have imagined. I recommend the Burris program highly.

Very Truly Yours, Lisa Watford

Lisa continues to use MIND/FITNESS with the students that she teaches privately today. This letter represents the big picture of MIND/FITNESS. It is a set of tools that will allow you to take control of your life and your children's life. Let's face it, everything that you have learned is not beneficial to you and everything that you teach your children is not beneficial to them. Does it not make sense then that you teach yourself and your children how to take control of what does not work? In other words, **unlearning** is as important as

learning. Teaching our children how to think independently is the best way to protect them and MIND/FITNESS is the tool to do that.

The reason the program process of MIND/FITNESS worked so well from the beginning is that Dr. Brenner was a statistician and from the beginning required that I set up the program to collect data. It was from this data collection that the process was formed and I simply refined the program day after day, year after year to conform to the people I was working with. I complied with the definition of insanity and never repeated something that did not work.

As you progress through this book you will come across the five key questions that you are instructed to ask yourself everyday. The first and most important question which I ask my clients to ask themselves everyday is: "Does this work for me?"

What determines your emotional state and eating behavior

All of this research and development led me back to the most fundamental question for anyone whom wants to initiate behavior change. What determines your emotional state and behavior, in particular your eating behavior? I have yet to come across anyone that can answer this question, yet this is the most fundamental question if you wish to initiate lasting permanent change. How can you move forward if you do not definitively know what is moving you forward. This single question is indicative of what is wrong with the current system of psychology.

If you can not answer this question, how could you possibly know how to help someone? I have worked with people who have had several years of psychotherapy and they can not answer this question. This has never been shocking to me because I have never come across a psychiatrist, psychologist or physician whom could answer it either.

What determines your emotional state and eating behavior is just **information**. Can you do anything in your life without talking to yourself or seeing a picture of what you need to do? Of course not! It would be a little bit like trying to read from a blank page. No information = no action!

The next question is: What are the components of this information? The components of the information that determines your emotional state and behavior are words and pictures.

The next logical question then is how do you **Recognize**, **Access** and **Change** the information that is driving a behavior that simply does not work?

This is where over 20 years of research and development come in with a program process now known as MIND/FITNESS. MIND/FITNESS answers the last question with great precision and accuracy by virtue of starting out with the first two questions. In the resolution of any problem it is always about the question. Never has this been more relevant. Imagine if for the last 60 years psychologists asked, "How can I fix it?" *instead of* "Why is it broken?!" Shortly you will discover why this small difference has more meaning than you ever realized.

Recognize

When eating or not eating becomes a behavior instead of a need to survive it is not unlike any other behavior disorder. The core issue is that you are emotionally out of control and you need to at some point decide if you want to change or fix the problem. This first step is called recognition. In order to fix any behavior you wish to change, you need to recognize the problem. This is where conventional forms of psychotherapy shine. The problem is that there is not usually a fix.

Someone who has spent two, five, ten years or more trying to fix a problem will usually consider it arrogant of anyone, in particular a psychologist or psychiatrist, to tell them what they need to do. Try telling someone suffering from anorexia to just eat or someone who is overweight to just cut back on their calories. Virtually one hundred percent of the eating disorders I have worked with have had at least one year of psychotherapy and the advice they get is to eat more or you need to stop throwing up. This is through the course of digging around for sexual abuse. If your life is at risk you usually understand what you need to do.

It is time to evolve to the next step and this is what this book is about. I have recognized for some time that the system and community of psychology is in need of a major overhaul. More than anyone, psychologists need to be held accountable. When was the last time your psychologist asked you: "Does this work for you?" This needs to be a primary question at every session. Please do not misunderstand these comments about the community of psychology. If it were not for this community and the medical community, you would not now have your hands on the most powerful program process for behavior change. I just think it is time for every psychologist and psychiatrist to own the results they are producing.

I did not mean to digress from the main point and that is, **your recognition of what you want to change.** If you are asking yourself the first key question every day ("Does this work for me?"), then you will eventually recognize something that you need to change. After you recognize what you need to change, then you write this down as your initial goal.

If you have been fighting and losing, does it not make sense to learn how to fight before you get into the ring again? If you can agree that it is just **information** that drives you, then you can get on to the next step which is how to access the information that is not working.

Access

After you recognize the behavior that does not work, you then need to gain access to it so that you can make a full on assault of that **information**. There is only one-way to effectively do this and that is to have an organized process that gets it on paper.

This is the reason my first two titles included a booklet and required you to interact. This book will also require you to interact with it. To put it in the most simplistic terms, you cannot effect change in anything unless you take some sort of action. Yes it is helpful to talk about things but in the end does just talking get the job done?

Gaining access to the subconscious starts with establishing what your goal is or what you wish to change in your life. **The next step is to document how you relate to yourself about this goal.** In other words how you communicate to yourself about it. This of course brings up a couple of questions. The first one is: Do you talk to yourself? Yes. Talking to yourself is the first component of information that determines your emotional state and behavior and it is important to find out how you speak to yourself especially in regard to a goal that you have set for yourself.

When you document how you speak to yourself, this allows you to establish where you have started, where you are going, and where you want to end up. Without documenting this information you are simply guessing. Access to subconscious information is afforded by simply responding to statements and questions about your goals. This is known as the Subconscious Perspective and is Step 2 of the program process of MIND/FITNESS.

Change

Once you understand how to recognize and access the information that does not work for you, the process of making an assault on this information is relatively simple. The first step is to evaluate your self-talk and determine whether or not it is a dialogue that is going to lead you to the goal you have chosen. If it is not, then you begin the process of restructuring your internal dialogue until you definitively know that it will take you in the direction you have chosen. There will be more about how your internal dialogue is generated in the next chapter. Right now I just want you to grasp the most fundamental components of MIND/FITNESS.

Burris MIND/FITNESS Defined

Now that you understand the most fundamental principles of MIND/FITNESS the definition of MIND/FITNESS will make a little more sense.

"Burris MIND/FITNESS is the clinically proven process of changing your subconscious programming to match your conscious goals." What does this mean? Have you ever made a New Year's resolution only to fall back into your old behavior? Consciously you know what you want to do and what you want to accomplish. Subconsciously, however, there is a program that has conveniently been repeating itself for probably a number of years and will not change or go away simply because consciously you have decided to do something else.

This is why there is a 98% fail rate for people who make the number one resolution every year to lose weight. Until you have at least a basic understanding of how to recognize, access, and change your subconscious programming, your chances of permanently changing any behavior are going to be low to zero.

To give you an idea of the power of the subconscious, you can speak at a rate of about two to three hundred words per minute. Your subconscious runs at a rate of about one thousand to twelve hundred words per minute which is about four times faster than what you can speak. This is why you can talk on the phone and perform other tasks like typing on the computer or driving a car because the subconscious is already programmed to do the other tasks.

You can look at the conscious mind and the subconscious mind like a tug of war with a vat of mud in the middle for whom ever loses. The conscious mind is one-person on one side against the subconscious, which are four people on the other side. If the conscious decides to move in a different direction like losing weight, increasing your fitness program, quitting smoking or any number of other things, it is usually a losing proposition because you are simply out numbered with information. This is why it is so difficult to attain spontaneous change. MIND/FITNESS is going to make sure you have the most people on your side in the tug of war.

MIND/FITNESS is based on the reality that all behavior is emotionally driven or in other words your emotional state = your behavior. How you feel about things you do will always determine whether you move toward them or not. Remember you will always move toward perceived pleasure and away from pain. The key component of any behavioral change program must include how to get control of your emotional state.

So what is the biggest difference between MIND/FITNESS and any other behavioral change program? The question MIND/FITNESS asks is: "How can I fix it?" *as opposed to* "Why is it broken?" **Example:** If you get a flat tire on your car, do you want to walk back down the road to find out why you got the flat or do you want to know how to fix it so that you can keep moving forward?

The question is: Do you want to analyze your stored **information** or do you want to change or destroy the **information** that is not working so that you can continue moving down the road? It is certainly not necessary to spend the last 40 years of your life analyzing the first 40 years of your life.

If you are responding to stored **information** then how do you **Recognize, Access** and **Change** this **information**? Once you understand the basics, you can begin to take control by making an assault on the very beginning of the process.

It is imperative that you understand how to take control of the subconscious because the mind is like a car without an off switch and an unknown driver, if you do not predetermine the destination. If you decide not drive it, it is going to drive itself or someone else may get in the seat and drive it for you. Someone else driving might be ok if you agree to where they are going but what if you do not like where they are going?

For the first eighteen years of your life someone else drove the car. This was usually with little or no consideration to the younger passengers. Almost every decision was made for you. You were told what to do, what to eat and learned how to react to any given situation. Most parents do not realize that they are programming their children from the very moment you enter the world and they are just passing along what their parents had taught them, good or bad.

There are also a tremendous number of variables that can occur in your initial programming that may have little to do with your parents. The bottom line still remains. Do you, at some point, want to drive or do you want to continue letting someone or something else drive?

2

Programming - Reprogramming

Learning - Unlearning

From the moment of birth your first emotional experiences establish your subconscious perceptions of the world. There is not a moment of the day or night that you are not affected by your emotions. More often than not it is your programmed emotional states, not logic that control your behavior. Therefore in order to apply the process of MIND/FITNESS you must first understand how your subconscious mind works.

Your subconscious mind flawlessly records everything you have ever seen, felt, smelled, heard, or tasted. Unfortunately it is not capable of interpreting the true meaning of the information it records. It simply takes the information it accumulates, and organizes it into individual programs that determine how you will respond to recurring circumstances in your daily life.

Once your subconscious mind has taken certain information and formed it into a program, it will devote its considerable power to the continuation of that program behavior or habit, regardless of the consequences.

Your subconscious programming can be useful. This is what allows you to do things automatically like drive a car, type a letter, or use a computer. If the subconscious did not store this information for you in the form of a program, you would not be able to do these things automatically. The disadvantage to this is that there are some subconscious programs that simply do not work.

At some point in your life you may have been programmed to eat poorly or to respond poorly to a certain situation or to link pleasure to things like smoking, drugs or alcohol. The dilemma later in life is how to change the behaviors that do not work for you.

There are two subconscious components that activate an emotional state, which in turn determines your behavior.

1) You must talk to yourself which usually begins with a question *and*

2) By asking yourself a question your subconscious mind will always give you an answer, which in turn produces a correlating picture.

It is from this subconscious picture that your emotional state is determined and in turn determines your behavior. A good example of this process is when a person is overweight; they constantly ask themselves negative questions like: "Why am I so fat?" *or* "How did I get so fat?" *or* "Why can't I lose this weight???"

By asking yourself these types of negative questions, your subconscious mind will produce negative answers such as: You are fat because you overeat or you overeat because you are stressed and for each of these negative answers the subconscious mind will produce a correlating picture of you as a fat person.

The mind now interprets these subconscious pictures, as how you should look, and devotes its tremendous power toward maintaining this body image. So you see, every time you ask yourself a question there is a correlating subconscious picture, which determines your emotional response. Through the process of MIND/FITNESS you will learn how to **Recognize, Access** and **Change** these two subconscious components.

Unlike your conscious mind, your subconscious mind is always active, it never sleeps. An example of this is when you ask yourself the question: What is that person's name? For the life of you, you cannot think of their name and then maybe an hour or two later or even the next day their picture and name pop into your mind. The reason for this is your subconscious mind was continuously working on the name, even though you had consciously given up.

If the subconscious does not already have a stored answer for a question, it will search through all of its available information until it formulates one. This is why you need to ask yourself any question you think may move you toward your weight goal because the subconscious will always find an answer.

It is estimated that your subconscious mind generates over 60 thousand thoughts per day. We refer to this thought process as talking to ourselves. The reason your subconscious mind is capable of generating over 60 thousand thoughts per day is because your inner voice continuously speaks to you at a rate of one thousand to twelve hundred words per minute. You can only speak however at about two to three hundred words per minute.

This means your inner voice runs at a rate of about four times faster than you can speak and produces a correlating picture for each of these thoughts. In other words if your mind was the world, your conscious mind might take up the space of LA or New York but your subconscious mind would take up the space and activity of the rest of the world.

Now that you have a better understanding of how your subconscious mind works and the power and control it has over your emotional state and behavior, I will now explain how your existing subconscious eating programs originated and why they remain so solidly locked in place.

Your Initial Programming

During the first part of your life you had no control: your parents did the majority of your thinking for you and in doing so created the greatest part of your subconscious programming. This is especially true in your eating behavior programming.

Your parents meant well but unfortunately they lacked the knowledge and the skills to instruct you on how to eat properly. They simply followed what their parents had taught them.

Does this sound familiar to you: "You are not going to leave the table until you finished everything on your plate." *or* "Do you realize there are children in the world who are starving and would give anything for your meal?" *or* "If you do not finish everything on your plate, there will be no dessert." It was these types of repetitive statements that programmed you to associate food with fear and guilt. What was really ironic, was when you grudgingly did manage to finish everything on your plate and were completely stuffed, you always managed to find room for your ultimate reward....a well-deserved dessert. With the consistent use of fear and guilt to control your behavior, eventually these two emotional states turned into anger, which also triggers emotional eating.

Now as an adult your worst eating behavior is perpetuated by the emotional states of fear, guilt and anger. The presence of these three emotional states also indicates the absence of your most positive and powerful emotional state, love.

Your parents used the reward of a dessert to control or program most of your emotional states. They knew that with the promise of something sweet, they could stop your anger, stop your crying, eliminate your boredom or stop your pain. If you want to train an animal, what do you use? You use food. Unfortunately human animals have full access to the very thing that was used to train many of their emotional states.

As a child you where unknowingly programmed to use eating as an outlet for practically all of your emotional states. Now that you are an adult you still emotionally respond to food exactly as you were programmed to do as a child. Your childhood programs still control why you eat, when you eat, what you eat, and how much you eat.

Anchored to your programming

Now that you know where and how your poor eating programs originated, I will explain why you keep repeating them over and over and what you must do to replace them with positive new programs.

The reason you keep repeating your childhood behaviors or habits over and over is because you are bonded or anchored to them. Yes, anchored as in weighted down or held in place! The only difference between your anchors and a ship anchor is your anchors do not consist of steel but are derived from your emotions.

Your anchors originated from extremely strong repetitive memory associations, which are triggered by your five senses of hearing, vision, smell, taste, and touch. You are constantly being anchored in different ways through out your life. For example, when you hear a certain song and it brings back a memory of a certain person, or a place in time, this is an audio anchor or an anchor triggered by your sense of hearing.

Have you ever met someone for the first time and noticed that something about them reminds you of someone or something else? This is a visual anchor or an anchor triggered by your sense of sight.

Until now all of your anchors have been installed in your subconscious mind by someone else or by accident and in most cases you were not even aware of them. Now for the first time through the process of MIND/FITNESS, you will learn how to anchor a reaction or behavior you want on purpose and consistently get the results you want over and over, until you are assured of attaining your weight goal.

It is important to understand that your subconscious mind can be triggered into a negative anchored behavior without even pausing to consider what it is doing. It is this type of behavior that is responsible for your worst eating habits. I refer to this type of behavior as "No Thought Eating." At the time of "No Thought Eating" your subconscious mind has given no consideration to what it is doing and your conscious mind is not even aware that anything is taking place.

A good example of this is when you are feeling fearful, guilty angry, or bored. You immediately look for something to eat, even if you are not hungry. In most cases you will look for what you refer to as your comfort foods, which is anything that is high in sugar, fat or both.

Let us say you come across a bag of cookies, without any hesitation you eat one and before you realize it, you are eating the whole bag. Sometime during this "No Thought Eating" binge your conscious mind awakens to what is taking place. You stop your eating binge and now along with feeling fearful, guilty, angry, or bored, you are also probably a little nauseous. The first thought that pops into your mind is: "Why Did I Eat That? I wasn't even hungry!" How many times have you asked yourself this self-defeating negative question "Why Did I Eat That?"

The second you asked yourself this question, your subconscious mind is triggered into action to find an answer, which in turn produces a correlating picture. Surprise, surprise what did it find in your subconscious eating behavior program? It found you ate the cookies because you were feeling fearful, guilty, angry, or bored. Of course it did because that is exactly how you were programmed as a child to react to fear, guilt, anger, or boredom. Once again your subconscious mind will take this answer and the correlating picture of you being overweight and use it to anchor you even deeper to your childhood program.

Programming your anchors

Here is where the fun starts, what do you have to do in order to change your existing negative anchored behaviors of "No Thought Eating?" You simply restructure your question from its negative form of "Why did I eat that?" to a positive form question of "How can I stop this no thought eating when I am feeling fearful, guilty, angry, or bored?" Your subconscious mind will now produce a positive answer to your new positive question such as: When you are feeling fearful, guilty, angry or bored, find an activity you enjoy in place of eating. Once again these new answers will produce empowering correlating pictures that will move you toward your weight goal. It is truly that simple, positive empowering questions = positive empowering results.

From this time on, it is essential that you are always conscious of your inner voice, thereby insuring that all of your self-questions are positive ones and insuring that you always maintain a positive emotional state.

Subconscious Pictures

Now that you understand how to affect change in your subconscious self-talk, let's now address the second component of MIND/ FITNESS, your subconscious pictures. I will explain how to replace your negative subconscious images into positive images through the practice of controlled visualization. According to the *New England Journal of Medicine*, visualizing is the fourth most frequently used form of alternative healing. You are now about to learn how to change your existing subconscious pictures that keep you anchored to your poor eating behavior.

Several studies have shown that the body makes little distinction between a vivid mental experience and an actual physical one. Your subconscious images are simply corresponding pictures of your self-talk.

Choosing to think in pictures may seem strange at first, but it is a powerful way to cut through the chatter in your head and a realistic source for communicating with your subconscious mind. It is surprisingly easy to develop your own weight-goal imagery. Through regular practice you will become more and more comfortable in delving into your imagination. Just think of it as creative constructive daydreaming.

Most people are not aware that there is always a corresponding picture for their thoughts or self-talk; the fact is they take place so fast you are not aware of them. If you did not use pictures, you would not be able to answer the simplest question. Think about it. If I were to ask you: "What did you have for breakfast this morning?" You immediately repeat my question to yourself which in turn triggers a picture in your subconscious mind of what you had for breakfast. It is only after you have triggered this picture that you are capable of answering my question.

You will find that your subconscious more clearly defines its pictures from questions than from statements. As an example, say to yourself body relax. You can see this has little or no effect. Now turn this statement into a question: What do I need to do to relax? The subconscious mind will now produce an active picture. For example, you might see yourself relaxing in your favorite chair or taking a warm soothing bath or possibly getting a massage. You are able to see the masseuse's expert hands gently soothe the tension from you body. You can feel the wonderful sensation as your body begins to relax and you feel as if you are floating on air. Now I am sure you understand the power of visualization and how you can use your self-questions to bring it about.

Your Most Important Internal Picture

The most important picture you will ever change in your subconscious mind is the picture you now have of your body or how you perceive your self-image. All people with a weight problem have accepted a picture of themselves as being overweight. Until you change this picture, your subconscious mind will use this existing body picture as a guideline for how you should look. This is why it is imperative that you change the image you have of yourself before you begin a weight loss program.

You will start your training in recreating subconscious imagery by recreating your existing body picture. Before starting your imagery training, it is important that you become totally relaxed in order to focus your mind. Once you have accomplished this, you will find it is quite easy to engage all of your senses, making it possible for you to create a new body image. Once you feel you are completely relaxed, I want you to see a picture of your body in your subconscious mind. When you have your body in focus, I want you to reshape it, to exactly how you want it to look.

See your new body down to the smallest detail; make it become so real that it seems that you have already accomplished your weight goal. Once you have your new body picture completed, place yourself in a physical activity that you know you would enjoy and will be beneficial in helping you attain your new weight goal. This activity can be anything from a brisk walk to an aerobics class, to playing tennis, to completing an unfinished task. Your new body is now capable of performing any activity that you find enjoyable.

Earlier I spoke about the emotional states that drive you to overeat or eat when you are not hungry. Fear, guilt and anger are responsible for the emotional states of depression and low self-esteem. When creating your new self-image, you must exchange these negative emotional states for your most powerful emotional state. Love is your most powerful emotional state especially when directed to your new self-image.

It is essential that you practice reproducing your new active body imagery on a daily basis. It is only through daily practice that your new body picture will become a permanent part of your subconscious, thus allowing you to reproduce this picture without a moments thought.

The power of MIND/FITNESS is in the ability to change programmed emotional states that do not work for you, for programmed emotional states that **DO** work for you.

Let's take a look at what you have learned in this chapter.

1) Your greatest power is the power of the word, especially when it is used in the form of a question to yourself.

2) MIND/FITNESS is based on the reality that all behavior is emotionally driven and the three key emotional states that drive you to overeat or eat when you are not hungry are fear, guilt and anger. Our most powerful emotional state is love.

3) There are two subconscious components that activate an emotional

state which in turn determines your eating behavior.

A) You must talk to yourself which usually begins with a question *and*

B) By asking yourself a question your subconscious mind will always give you an answer which in turn produces a correlating picture. It is from this subconscious picture that your emotional state is determined and in turn decides your eating behavior.

4) The most affective means of changing your self talk is to intervene and change your negative self questioning into positive empowering questions.

5) The most important subconscious image you have to change in order to attain and maintain your weight goal and take control of your eating behavior is the image you have of yourself right now.

The bottom line is that you must maintain awareness of your subconscious processes so that you can take your conscious goals and turn them into empowering subconscious programs. It is important to understand that all the resources you need to attain a permanent weight loss are stored right between your ears. All you have to do is learn what questions to ask yourself to achieve the results you want. **Ask and ye shall receive.**

3

Attacking the Body

To Try and Change the Mind

In the 27 years of my involvement in the health and fitness industry, I have never come across anyone that has focused their attention on the core of the problem of weight loss or eating disorders. Even though everything begins and ends with the mind, the assault was and still is on the body.

None of my clients has ever said to me, "Gee I did not realize that eating an entire cheesecake would make me fat." Yet the most popular weight loss programs continue with the assumption that people do not know that eating an entire apple pie with a half-gallon of vanilla ice cream is the cause for their obesity.

Most people that I have worked with consider it incredibly arrogant of a dietician, doctor, or psychologist that just by virtue of telling them to cut back on their sweets that they are immediately going to comply.

This mentality among the so-called weight loss professionals has driven the weight loss industry to an astounding 33 billion dollars a year. Conspiracy theorists should have a great time with this one. After all it does seem as though every diet and weight loss program out there is custom designed to not only fail but also dramatically increase the problem. This in turn increases revenues for the weight loss industry.

You cannot talk about the obscene failure of the weight loss industry without talking about the current system of psychology. Virtually all of my weight loss and eating disorder clients have had at least some psychological counseling. The more psychological counseling a client has had, the more difficult my job is because this becomes part of what the client must unlearn.

It is important to understand how you are evaluated as part of the statistical populace of the overweight and obese and to get a better understanding of where you are physically right now. This will help you determine what your goals need to be. This is also helpful if you are using this book to try and help someone else, and you need to get a clear picture of the problem. Either way, you need to have a view of the results of **Attacking the Body to Try and Change the Mind.**

Understanding BMI (Body Mass Index)

Because BMI does not show the difference between fat and muscle, it does not always accurately predict when weight could lead to health problems. For example, I weigh approximately 182 pounds and I am 6' 1" tall. I am between 10 and 12 percent body fat. This puts me at a BMI of 24. This is within range but only one point away of what the BMI chart considers overweight. If you are sedentary and you know you are out of shape and overweight, then this chart has a lot more relevance.

BMI also may also not accurately reflect body fatness in people who are very short (under 5 feet), in older people who tend to lose muscle mass as they age, and women who are pregnant. For most people, however, BMI is a reliable way to tell if your weight is putting your health at risk.

Following is a BMI chart, BMI formula and a BMI table.

Classification of Overweight and Obesity by BMI
< = Less Than   > = Greater than

	Obesity Class	BMI
Underweight		<18.5
Normal		18.5 - 24.9
Overweight		25.0 - 29.9
Obesity	I	30.0 - 34.9
	II	35.0 - 39.9
Extreme Obesity	III	≥40

BMI Formula

BMI =	$\dfrac{\text{Weight in Pounds}}{\text{(Height in inches) x (Height in inches)}}$	X 703

For BMI calculators go to www.NIH.gov. When you get there, type in BMI in the search box, and you will get a list of BMI calculators.

The BMI Table

To use the table, find the appropriate height in the left-hand column labeled Height. Move across the right to a given weight. The number at the top of the column is the BMI at that height and weight. Pounds have been rounded off.

BMI Table

BMI	19	20	21	22	23	24	25	26	27	28	29	Weight (Pounds)
Height (Inches)												
58	91	96	100	105	110	115	119	124	129	134	138	
59	94	99	104	109	114	119	124	128	133	138	143	
60	97	102	107	112	118	123	128	133	138	143	148	
61	100	106	111	116	122	127	132	137	143	148	153	
62	104	109	115	120	126	131	136	142	147	153	158	
63	107	113	118	124	130	135	141	146	152	158	163	
64	110	116	122	128	134	140	145	151	157	163	169	
65	114	120	126	132	138	144	150	156	162	168	174	
66	118	124	130	136	142	148	155	161	167	173	179	
67	121	127	134	140	146	153	159	166	172	178	185	
68	125	131	138	144	151	158	164	171	177	184	190	
69	128	135	142	149	155	162	169	176	182	189	196	
70	132	139	146	153	160	167	174	181	188	195	202	
71	136	143	150	157	165	172	179	186	193	200	208	
72	140	147	154	162	169	177	184	191	199	206	213	
73	144	151	159	166	174	182	189	197	204	212	219	
74	148	155	163	171	179	186	194	202	210	218	225	
75	152	160	168	176	184	192	200	208	216	224	232	
76	156	164	172	180	189	197	205	213	221	230	238	

BMI Table Continued

BMI	30	31	32	33	34	35	36	37	38	39	40	Weight (Pounds)
Height (Inches)												
58	143	148	153	158	162	167	172	177	181	186	191	
59	148	153	158	163	168	173	178	183	188	193	198	
60	153	158	163	168	174	179	184	189	194	199	204	
61	158	164	169	174	180	185	190	195	201	206	211	
62	164	169	175	180	186	191	196	202	207	213	218	
63	169	175	180	186	191	197	203	208	214	220	225	
64	174	180	186	192	197	204	209	215	221	227	232	
65	180	186	192	198	204	210	216	222	228	234	240	
66	186	192	198	204	210	216	223	229	235	241	247	
67	191	198	204	211	217	223	230	236	242	249	255	
68	197	204	210	216	223	230	236	243	249	256	262	
69	203	210	216	223	230	236	243	250	257	263	270	
70	209	216	222	229	236	243	250	257	264	271	278	
71	215	222	229	236	243	250	257	265	272	279	286	
72	221	228	235	242	250	258	265	272	279	287	294	
73	227	235	242	250	257	265	272	280	288	295	302	
74	233	241	249	256	264	272	280	287	295	303	311	
75	240	248	256	264	272	279	287	295	303	311	319	
76	246	254	263	271	279	287	295	304	312	320	328	

Obesity Statistics – Understanding the Problem

Approximately 300,000 adult deaths in the United States each year are attributable to unhealthy dietary habits and physical inactivity or sedentary behavior.[7]   This statistic is second only to cigarette smokers who die at a rate of 440,000 per year.

Following are some frequently asked questions and answers about overweight and obesity statistics. Data are based on NHANES 1999-2000. NHANES is the National Health and Nutrition Examination Survey. This is part of the Center for Disease Control and Prevention (or CDC). Unless otherwise specified, the figures given represent age-adjusted estimates. Population numbers are based on the U.S. Census Bureau *Census 2000.*

Can you trust these numbers? Any time data is collected there are going to variables. There will be arguments about these numbers, and there are inherent problems with the BMI chart. You need to know how to use the BMI index because this is what the CDC and NIH uses along with many other agencies that do extensive research on the affects of obesity.

Unless otherwise specified, the figures given represent total (not age-adjusted) numbers. The statistics presented here are based on the following definitions unless otherwise specified: overweight = BMI 25 to greater than 30; obesity = BMI 30. One of the questions I get is can't you be fat and healthy. If your BMI is 30 or higher, the simple answer is no. The following Questions and Answers should help you gain a clearer perspective.

Questions and Answers about obesity

Q: How many adults are overweight?

A: Nearly two-thirds of U.S. adults are overweight (BMI $\geq$ 25, which includes those who are obese).[8]

All adults (20+ years old):	129.6 million (64.5 percent)
Women (20+ years old):	64.5 million (61.9 percent)
Men (20+ years old):	65.1 million (67.2 percent)

Q: How many adults are obese?

A: Nearly one-third of U.S. adults are obese (BMI $\geq$ 30).[8]

All adults (20+ years old):	61.3 million (30.5 percent)
Women (20+ years old):	34.7 million (33.4 percent)
Men (20+ years old):	26.6 million (27.5 percent)

Q: How many adults are at a healthy weight?

A: Less than half of U.S. adults have a healthy weight (BMI $\geq$ 18.5 to < 25).[9]

All adults (20-74 years old):	67.3 million (33.5 percent)
Women (20-74 years old):	36.7 million (35.3 percent)
Men (20-74 years old):	30.6 million (31.8 percent)

Q: How has the prevalence of overweight and obesity in adults changed over the years?

A: The prevalence has steadily increased over the years among both genders, all ages, all racial/ethnic groups, all educational levels, and all smoking levels.

From 1960 to 2000, the prevalence of overweight (BMI $\geq$ 25 to < 30) increased from 31.5 to 33.6 percent in U.S. adults aged 20 to 74.[9] The prevalence of obesity (BMI $\geq$ 30) during this same time period more than doubled from 13.3 to 30.9 percent, with most of this rise occurring in the past 20 years. From 1988 to 2000, the prevalence of extreme obesity (BMI ≥ 40) increased from 2.9 to 4.7 percent, up from 0.8 percent in 1960.3,8. In 1991, four states had obesity rates of 15 percent or higher, and none had obesity rates above 16 percent. By 2000, every state except Colorado had obesity rates of 15 percent or more, and 22 states had obesity rates of 20 percent or more.[11] The prevalence of overweight and obesity generally increases with advancing age, then starts to decline among people over 60.[3]

Q: What is the prevalence of overweight and obesity in minorities?
A: The age-adjusted prevalence of combined overweight and obesity (BMI ≥ 25) in racial/ethnic minorities—especially minority women—is generally higher than in whites in the United States.[8]

Non-Hispanic Black women:	77.3%
MexicanAmerican women:	71.9%
Non-Hispanic White women:	57.3%
Non-Hispanic Black men:	60.7%
Mexican American men:	74.7%
Non-Hispanic White men:	67.4%

(Statistics are for populations 20+ years old)

Studies using this definition of overweight and obesity provide ethnicity-specific data only for these three racial-ethnic groups. Studies using definitions of overweight and obesity from NHANES II have reported a high prevalence of overweight and obesity among Hispanics and American Indians. The prevalence of overweight (BMI ≥ 25) and obesity (BMI ≥ 30) in Asian Americans is lower than in the population as a whole.[1]

The continued increase in overweight among America's children demands attention and calls for action," said Dr. Edward J. Sondik, Director of the National Center for Health Statistics,

Centers for Disease Control and Prevention. "Our children learn by example, so as a nation, we all need to adopt healthier diets and become more physically active," he said. (Did he just say we are programming our children to be fat?)

The report stated that the reasons for the increase in overweight were not clear but suggested that eating out, diets low in fruits and vegetables, and lack of exercise probably play a role.

Q: What is the prevalence of overweight and obesity in children and adolescents?

A: While there is no generally accepted definition for *obesity* as distinct from *overweight* in children and adolescents, the prevalence of *overweight** is increasing for children and adolescents in the United States. Approximately 15.3 percent of children (ages 6–11) and 15.5 percent of adolescents (ages 12–19) were overweight in 2000. An additional 15 percent of children and 14.9 percent of adolescents were at risk for overweight (BMI for age between the 85th and 95th percentile).[12]

Q: What is the prevalence of diabetes in people who are overweight or obese?

A: Among people diagnosed with type 2 (non insulin-dependent) diabetes, 67 percent have a BMI ≥ 27 and 46 percent have a BMI ≥ 30.[14] About 17 million people in the U.S. have type 2 diabetes, accounting for more than 90 percent of diabetes cases.[15] An additional 20 million have impaired glucose tolerance, sometimes called pre-diabetes, which is a strong risk factor for developing diabetes later in life. An estimated 70 percent of diabetes risk in the U.S. can be attributed to excess weight.[16]

Q: What is the prevalence of hypertension (high blood pressure) in people who are overweight or obese?

A: The age-adjusted prevalence of hypertension in overweight U.S. adults is 22.1 percent for men with BMI ≥ 25 and < 27; 27.0 percent for men with BMI ≥ 27 and < 30; 27.7 percent for women with BMI ≥ 25 and < 27; and 32.7 percent for women BMI ≥ 27 and < 30. In comparison, the prevalence of hypertension in adults who are not overweight (BMI <25) is 14.9 percent for men and 15.2 percent for women. The prevalence in adults who are obese (BMI ≥ 30) is 41.9 percent for men and 37.8 percent for women.17 (Hypertension is defined as mean systolic blood pressure ≥ 140 mm Hg, mean diastolic ≥ 90 mm Hg, or currently taking antihypertensive medication.)

Q: What is the prevalence of high blood cholesterol in people who are overweight or obese?

A: The age-adjusted prevalence of high blood cholesterol (≥ 240 mg/dL) in overweight U.S. adults is 19.1 percent for men with BMI ≥ 25 and < 27; 21.6 percent for men with BMI ≥ 27 and < 30; 30.5 percent for women with BMI ≥ 25 and < 27; and 29.6 percent for women BMI ≥ 27 and < 30. In comparison, the prevalence of high cholesterol in adults who are not overweight (BMI <25) is 13.0 percent for men and 13.4 percent for women. The prevalence for adults who are obese (BMI ≥ 30) is 22.0 percent for men and 27.0 percent for women. [17]

Q: What is the prevalence of cancer in people who are overweight or obese?

A: While direct prevalence information is not available, a recent study found that people whose BMI was 40 or more had death rates from cancer that were 52 percent higher for men and 62 percent higher for women than rates for normal-weight men and women. Overweight and obesity could account for 14 percent of cancer deaths among men and 20 percent among women in the U.S. In both men and women, higher BMI is associated with higher death rates from cancers of the esophagus, colon and rectum, liver, gallbladder, pancreas, and kidney. The same trend applies to cancers of the stomach and prostate in men and cancers of the breast, uterus, cervix, and ovaries in women. [18] Almost half of post-menopausal women diagnosed with breast cancer have a BMI ≥ 29.19 In one study (the Nurses' Health Study), women gaining more than 20 pounds from age 18 to midlife doubled their risk of breast cancer, compared to women whose weight remained stable. [20]

Q: What is the mortality rate associated with obesity?

A: Most studies show an increase in mortality rate associated with obesity (BMI ≥ 30). Obese individuals have a 50 to 100 percent increased risk of death from all causes, compared with normal-weight individuals (BMI 20–25). Most of the increased risk is due to cardiovascular causes. [21] Life expectancy of a moderately obese person could be shortened by 2 to 5 years. White men between 20 and 30 years old with a BMI ≥ 45 could shorten their life expectancy by 13 years; white women in the same category could lose up to 8 years of life. Young African American men with a BMI ≥ 45 could lose up to 20 years of life; African American women, up to 5.[22]

As the prevalence of overweight and obesity has increased in the United States, so have related health care costs—both direct and indirect. Direct health care costs refer to preventive, diagnostic, and treatment services (for example, physician visits, medications, and hospital and nursing home care). Indirect costs are the value of wages lost by people unable to work because of illness or disability, as well as the value of future earnings lost by premature death.

Most of the statistics presented below represent the economic cost of overweight and obesity in the United States in 1995, updated to 2001 dollars.[23] Unless otherwise noted, the statistics given are adapted from Wolf and Colditz [24], who based their data on existing epidemiological studies that defined overweight and obesity as a BMI ≥ 29. Because the prevalence of overweight and obesity has increased since 1995, the costs today are higher than the figures given here.

Q: What is the cost of overweight and obesity?
A: Total cost: $122.9 billion
   Direct cost: $64.1 billion *
   Indirect cost: $58.8 billion
   (comparable to the economic costs of cigarette smoking)

Q: What is the cost of heart disease related to overweight and obesity?
A: Direct cost: $8.8 billion (17 percent of the total direct cost of heart disease, independent of stroke)

Q: What is the cost of type 2 diabetes related to overweight and obesity?
A: Total cost: $98 billion (in 2001)[16]

Q: What is the cost of osteoarthritis related to overweight and obesity?
A: Total cost: $21.2 billion
   Direct cost: $5.3 billion
   Indirect cost: $15.9 billion

Q: What is the cost of hypertension (high blood pressure) related to overweight and obesity?

A: Direct cost: $4.1 billion (17 percent of the total cost of hypertension)

Q: What is the cost of gallbladder disease related to overweight and obesity?

A: Total cost: $3.4 billion
   Direct cost: $3.2 billion
   Indirect cost: $187 million

Q: What is the cost of cancer related to overweight and obesity?

A: Breast cancer: Total cost: $2.9 billion; Direct cost: $1.1 billion; Indirect cost: $1.8 billion

Endometrial cancer: Total cost: $933 million; Direct cost: $310 million; Indirect cost: $623 million

Colon cancer: Total cost: $3.5 billion; Direct cost: $1.3 billion; Indirect cost: $2.2 billion

Q: What is the cost of lost productivity related to obesity?

A: The cost of lost productivity related to obesity (BMI $\geq$ 30) among Americans ages 17–64 is $3.9 billion. This value considers the following annual numbers (for 1994):

   Workdays lost related to obesity: 39.3 million
   Physician office visits related to obesity: 62.7 million
   Restricted activity days related to obesity: 239.0 million
   Bed-days related to obesity: 89.5 million

Q: How much do we spend on weight-loss products and services?

A: Americans spend $33 billion annually on weight-loss products and services.[26] (This figure represents consumer dollars spent in the early 1990's on all efforts at weight loss or weight maintenance including low-calorie foods, artificially sweetened products such as diet sodas, and memberships to commercial weight-loss centers).

Q: How physically active is the U.S. population?

A: Less than one-third (31.8 percent) of U.S. adults get regular leisure-time physical activity (defined as light or moderate activity five times or more per week for 30 minutes or more each time and/or vigorous activity three times or more per week for 20 minutes or more each time). About 10 percent of adults do no physical activity at all in their leisure time. [27]

About 25 percent of young people (ages 12–21 years) participate in light to moderate activity (e.g., walking, bicycling) nearly every day. About 50 percent regularly engage in vigorous physical activity. Approximately 25 percent report no vigorous physical activity, and 14 percent report no recent vigorous or light to moderate physical activity.[28]

Q: What is the cost of lack of physical activity?

A: The direct cost of physical inactivity may be as high as $24.3 billion. [29]

Q: What are the benefits of physical activity?

A: In addition to helping to control weight, physical activity decreases the risk of dying from coronary heart disease and reduces the risk of developing diabetes, hypertension, and colon cancer. [28]

Please see the Bibliography at the end of the book for recourses for this chapter.

4

When Does Eating Become a Disorder

By the time I see a client for an eating disorder, they have usually been diagnosed. There are criteria that have been set by National Institute of Mental Health (NIMH) and Harvard Eating Disorders Center. These criteria cover all eating disorders.

When we think of eating disorders, we usually think of a young woman who is either starving herself or throwing up or both. Karen Carpenter is probably the image most people identify with as someone with an eating disorder. Very few people view someone who is obese as someone with an eating disorder. Obesity, however, is definitely but not always part of the equation. This demographic is much more difficult to define than someone who starves themselves or vomits after eating.

Eating disorders frequently co-occur with other psychiatric disorders such as depression, substance abuse, and anxiety disorders. I have found that the demographic for binge eating disorders have a much wider range than anorexia nervosa or bulimia nervosa.

Following is a question and answer for binge eating disorder, anorexia nervosa, and bulimia. This will help you more clearly define where you are so that you can more accurately determine where you need to go. The following questions and answers are only designed to establish a basic knowledge of eating disorders and disordered eating. If you think you have an eating disorder, you need to make an appointment with someone who is qualified to accurately diagnose you.

Binge Eating Disorder Question and Answers

Q: How do I know if I have a Binge Eating Disorder?
A: Most of us overeat from time to time, and many people often feel they've eaten more than they should have. Eating a lot of food does not always mean that a person has binge eating disorder. Doctors generally agree that most people with serious binge eating problems often:
  • Feel their eating is out of control
  • Eat what most people would think is an unusually large amount of food
  • Eat much more quickly than usual during binge episodes
  • Eat until so full they are uncomfortable
  • Eat large amounts of food, even when they are not really hungry
  • Eat alone because they are embarrassed about the amount of food they eat
  • Feel disgusted, depressed, or guilty after overeating

Binge eating also takes place in another eating disorder called *bulimia nervosa*. Persons with bulimia nervosa, however, usually purge, fast, or do strenuous exercise after they binge eat. *Purging* means vomiting or using a lot of diuretics (water pills) or laxatives to keep from gaining weight. *Fasting* is not eating for at least 24 hours. *Strenuous exercise,* in this case, means exercising for more than an hour just to keep from gaining weight after binge eating. Purging, fasting, and over exercising are dangerous ways to try to control your weight.

Q: How common is Binge Eating Disorder?

A: Binge eating disorder is probably the most common eating disorder. Most people with this problem are either overweight or obese, but normal-weight people also can have the disorder.

About 2 percent of all adults in the United States (as many as 4 million Americans) have binge eating disorder. About 10 to 15 percent of people who are mildly obese and who try to lose weight on their own or through commercial weight-loss programs have binge eating disorder. The disorder is even more common in people who are severely obese.

Binge eating disorder is a little more common in women than in men; three women for every two men have it. The disorder affects blacks as often as whites. No one knows how often it affects people in other ethnic groups.

People who are obese and have binge eating disorder often became overweight at a younger age than those without the disorder. They might also lose and gain back weight (yo-yo diet) more often.

Q: What causes Binge Eating Disorder?

A: No one knows for sure what causes binge eating disorder. As many as half of all people with binge eating disorder have been depressed in the past. Whether depression causes binge eating disorder or whether binge eating disorder causes depression is not known.

Many people who are binge eaters say that being angry, sad, bored, or worried can cause them to binge eat. Impulsive behavior (acting quickly without thinking) and certain other emotional problems can be more common in people with binge eating disorder.

It is also unclear if dieting and binge eating are related. Some studies show that about half of all people with binge eating disorder had binge episodes before they started to diet.

Researchers also are looking into how brain chemicals and metabolism (the way the body uses calories) affect binge eating disorder. This research is still in the early stages.

Q: What are the complications of Binge Eating Disorder?

A: People with binge eating disorder can get sick because they may not be getting the right nutrients. They usually eat large amounts of fats and sugars, which don't have a lot of vitamins or minerals. People with binge eating disorder are usually very upset by their binge eating and may become very depressed.

People who are obese and also have binge eating disorder are at risk for:

- Diabetes
- High blood pressure
- High blood cholesterol levels
- Gallbladder disease
- Heart disease
- Certain types of cancer

Most people with binge eating disorder have tried to control it on their own, but they have not been able to control it for very long. Some people miss work, school, or social activities to binge eat. Persons who are obese with binge eating disorder often feel bad about themselves and may avoid social gatherings.

Q: Should people with Binge Eating Disorder try to diet?

A: People who are not overweight should avoid dieting because it sometimes makes their binge eating worse. Dieting here means skipping meals, not eating enough food each day, or avoiding certain kinds of food (such as carbohydrates). These are unhealthy ways to try to change your body shape and weight. Many people with binge eating disorder are obese and have health problems because of their weight. These people should try to lose weight and keep it off.

People with binge eating disorder who are obese may find it harder to stay in a weight-loss program. They also may lose less weight than other people and may regain weight more quickly. (This can be worse when they also have problems like depression, trouble controlling their behavior, and problems dealing with other people.) These people may need treatment for binge eating disorder before they try to lose weight.

Anorexia Nervosa Defined

Anorexia Nervosa is a serious, potentially life-threatening eating disorder characterized by self-starvation and excessive weight loss.

Anorexia Nervosa has four primary symptoms

- Resistance to maintaining body weight at or above a minimally normal weight for age and height.
- Intense fear of weight gain or being "fat" even though underweight.
- Disturbance in the experience of body weight or shape, undue influence of weight or shape on self-evaluation, or denial of the seriousness of low body weight.
- Loss of menstrual periods in girls and women post-puberty.

Warning Signs of Anorexia Nervosa

- Dramatic weight loss.
- Preoccupation with weight, food, calories, fat grams, and dieting.
- Refusal to eat certain foods, progressing to restrictions against whole categories of food (e.g. no carbohydrates, etc.).
- Frequent comments about feeling "fat" or overweight despite weight loss.
- Anxiety about gaining weight or being "fat."
- Denial of hunger.
- Development of food rituals (e.g. eating foods in certain orders, excessive chewing, rearranging food on a plate).
- Consistent excuses to avoid mealtimes or situations involving food.
- Excessive, rigid exercise regimen—despite weather, fatigue, illness, or injury—the need to "burn off" calories taken in.
- Withdrawal from usual friends and activities.
- In general, behaviors and attitudes indicating that weight loss, dieting, and control of food are becoming primary concerns.

Bulimia Nervosa Defined

Bulimia Nervosa is a serious, potentially life-threatening eating disorder characterized by a cycle of bingeing and compensatory behaviors such as self-induced vomiting designed to undo or compensate for the effects of binge eating.

Bulimia Nervosa has three primary symptoms

- Regular intake of large amounts of food accompanied by a sense of loss of control over eating behavior.

- Regular use of inappropriate compensatory behaviors such as self-induced vomiting, laxative or diuretic abuse, fasting, and/or obsessive or compulsive exercise.
- Extreme concern with body weight and shape.

Eating-disorder specialists believe that the chance for recovery increases the earlier bulimia nervosa is detected. Therefore, it is important to be aware of some of the warning signs of bulimia nervosa.

Warning Signs of Bulimia Nervosa

- Evidence of binge-eating, including disappearance of large amounts of food in short periods of time or the existence of wrappers and containers indicating the consumption of large amounts of food.
- Evidence of purging behaviors, including frequent trips to the bathroom after meals, signs and/or smells of vomiting, presence of wrappers or packages of laxatives or diuretics.
- Excessive, rigid exercise regimen—despite weather, fatigue, illness, or injury—the need to "burn off" calories taken in.
- Unusual swelling of the cheeks or jaw area.
- Calluses on the back of the hands and knuckles from self-induced vomiting.
- Discoloration or staining of the teeth.
- Creation of complex lifestyle schedules or rituals to make time for binge-and-purge sessions.
- Withdrawal from usual friends and activities.
- In general, behaviors and attitudes indicating that weight loss, dieting, and control of food are becoming primary concerns.

How to determine if you have an Eating Disorder

Disordered eating refers to mild and transient changes in eating patterns that occur in relation to a stressful event, an illness, or even a desire to modify the diet for a variety of health and personal appearance reasons. The problem may be no more than a bad habit, a style of eating adapted from friends or family members, or an aspect of preparing for athletic competition.

While disordered eating can lead to weight loss or weight gain and to certain nutritional problems, it rarely requires in-depth professional attention. On the other hand, disordered eating can develop into an eating disorder. If disordered eating becomes sustained, distressing, or starts to interfere with everyday activities, then it may require professional evaluation.

Given Americans' interest in being fit and the widespread practice of dieting, it can sometimes be difficult to tell where disordered eating stops and an eating disorder begins. Indeed, many eating disorders get their start from a simple diet or inadvertent weight loss.

It is known that disordered eating or dieting can precipitate an eating disorder, and it is important to understand that when we talk of an eating disorder, we are talking about an illness. Eating disorders involve physiological changes associated with food restricting, binge eating, purging, and fluctuations in weight. They also involve a number of **emotional** and **cognitive** changes that affect the way a person perceives and experiences his or her body.

An eating disorder is not a diet, a sign of personal weakness, or a problem that will go away by itself. An eating disorder requires immediate attention.

Disordered Eating vs. Eating Disorders

	Disordered Eating	**Eating Disorders**
Essential Distinction	A reaction to life situations. A habit.	An illness.
Psychological Symptoms	Infrequent thoughts and behaviors about body, foods, and eating that do not lead to health, social, school, and work problems.	Frequent and persistent thoughts and behaviors about body, foods, and eating that do lead to health, social, school, and work problems
Associated Medical Problems	May lead to transient weight changes or nutritional problems; rarely causes major medical complications.	Can result in major medical complications that lead to hospitalization or even death.
Treatment	Education and/or self-help group can assist with change. Psychotherapy and nutritional counseling can be helpful but are not usually essential.	Requires specific professional medical and mental health treatment. Problem does not go away without treatment.

Eating Disorder Statistics

Eating disorders have reached epidemic levels in America:
All segments of society, young and old, rich and poor, all minorities,
including African American and Latino.
Seven million women
One million men

Age at onset of illness

86% report onset of illness by the age of 20*
10% report onset at 10 years or younger
33% report onset between ages of 11-15
43% report onset between ages of 16-20

Duration of Illness/Mortality

77% report duration from one to fifteen years*
30% report duration from one to five years
31% report duration from six to ten years
16% report duration from eleven to fifteen years
It is estimated that six percent of serious cases die
Only 50% report being cured

Cost of Treatment

Treatment for anorexia nervosa and/or bulimia is often extremely
expensive.

Large numbers of victims require extensive medical monitoring and
treatment, and therapy generally extends over two years or more.

Cost of inpatient treatment can be $30,000 or more a month. Many patients need repeated hospitalizations.

The cost of outpatient treatment, including therapy and medical monitoring, can extend to $100,000 or more.

Eating disorders are rampant in our society; yet, few states in the nation have adequate programs or services to combat eating disorders such as anorexia nervosa and bulimia. Only a small number of schools and colleges have programs to educate our youth about the dangers of eating disorders.

Every state in our nation and thousands of schools has extensive programs aimed to prevent alcoholism and drug abuse. The value of such programs, especially education programs, has been proven and accepted into school curricula.

The immense suffering surrounding eating disorders, the high cost of treatment, and the longevity of these illnesses make it imperative that vastly expanded education programs be implemented to prevent anorexia nervosa and related disorders.

Since 86 percent of victims report the onset of their illness by age 20, education programs should focus on these ages in order to maximize preventive efforts.

* ANAD Ten Year Study – (National Association of Anorexia Nervosa and Associated Disorders)

No Standardized Approach

There are over 400 schools of psychotherapy, each claiming a distinct theory and set of treatment techniques. Psychodynamic and cognitive-behavioral therapies probably represent the most widely used.

There is no one definitive form of therapy recommended for eating disorders. Often the therapist will evaluate the status of the patient. For some individuals, they may be very knowledgeable and have had experience with some intervention. For others, it is a totally new experience.

Most often a supportive psycho-educational format launches the process. Most therapists will either combine or progress to a cognitive-behavioral or psychodynamic approach.

Not having a standardized form of treatment for eating disorders is a huge problem; the fact that therapists mix and match their treatment is troubling to say the least. This is the only business I am aware of that is not required to produce any results. In fact many times just the opposite is true.

In the process of compiling the program process of MIND/FITNESS, I worked with many bright, well-educated, caring psychologists who lived their lives to make a difference and even made attempts to incorporate MIND/FITNESS into the facilities in which they worked but were forced to comply within the framework of their corporate structure. The problem within our system of psychology is not the therapist, but the structure in which they are required to work. Does it make any sense to go to someone whose training does not give them the tools to fix themselves?

What about the use of psychoanalysis or conventional psychology to help make a behavioral change? You need to ask yourself what results you want from a particular behavioral issue you wish to address. Do you want to know why you do what you do—or do you want to fix it?

Do you ever hear something different than what a person is actually saying? This is what I experience with conventional psychology. You walk into the psychologist office and the psychologist says to you: "First we will find out what the problem is and then we will make you feel better." What I hear him saying is: "First I would like to drag you through the junkyard of your past and then we'll find someone to blame it on."

I am not saying that psychology is wrong for everyone. I am just saying that you need to know the results that you want before you begin speaking to someone about a problem. The fact that Freud developed psychoanalysis in the late 1800s when few people knew what indoor plumbing was and we were scooping up the pollution from our transportation with a shovel, does influence this opinion.

If you want to change a behavior or have some reasonable level of control over what you are doing, then MIND/FITNESS is the answer. How can I say this with such confidence? I have documented clinical studies that have proven the empowering benefits of MIND/FITNESS over and over again.

Everything in Burris MIND/FITNESS is looked at as an accomplishment. In other words, if you are 50 pounds overweight, you had to do something to accomplish this. The question now is how can you undo this? This is where the big difference between conventional psychology and MIND/FITNESS shows up. Conventional psychological focus will be on what motivated the behavior. Was it your father, your mother, an aunt, an uncle, or just a traumatic experience?

The focus of MIND/FITNESS is how you accomplished this. Notice I said you. That's right; when I work with someone, I do not need or want any background history. I simply want to know what process you went through to accomplish the current state that you want to change. In other words, what process did the mind go through to help you accomplish and maintain your current emotional state and behavior?

Following is a comparison between Burris MIND/FITNESS (BMF) and Cognitive-Behavioral Therapy. I chose Cognitive-Behavioral Therapy (CBT) because I believe this to be the most advanced and most useful of any of the psychotherapies used today.

Burris MIND/FITNESS Versus Cognitive-Behavioral Therapy

CBT is based on the Cognitive Model of Emotional Response. Cognitive-behavioral therapy is based on the scientific fact that our *thoughts* cause our feelings and behaviors, not external things like people, situations, and events. The benefit of this fact is that we can change the way we think to feel/act better even if the situation has not changed.

Burris MIND/FITNESS

Burris MIND/FITNESS is the clinically proven process of changing your subconscious programming to match your conscious goals.

BMF is based on the reality that all behavior is emotionally driven so if you understand how an emotional state comes about, you can intervene and change the behavior. BMF is not psychotherapy; it is a **program process**.

Cognitive-Behavioral Therapy

CBT is Briefer and Time-Limited. Cognitive-behavioral therapy is considered among the "fastest" in terms of results obtained. The average number of sessions clients receive (across all types of problems) is only 16. Other forms of therapy, like psychoanalysis, can take years. What enables CBT to be briefer is its highly instructional nature and the fact that it makes use of homework assignments.

Burris MIND/FITNESS

BMF has been used since 1990, as a one or two session fix depending on the time the client wants to spend per session. A single session fix will take approximately 4 hours. Upon completion of the program process, the client has all the tools necessary to initiate another assault should the client relapse and the emotional state and behavior return.

Cognitive-Behavioral Therapy

A sound therapeutic relationship is necessary for effective therapy, but not the focus. Some forms of therapy assume that the main reason people get better in therapy is because of the positive relationship between the therapist and client. Cognitive-behavioral therapists believe it is important to have a good, trusting relationship, but that is not enough. CBT therapists believe that the client changes when they learn to think differently; therefore, CBT therapists focus on teaching rational self-counseling skills.

Burris MIND/FITNESS

Rapport is an important key in the program process of BMF. Like CBT rapport is not the primary factor but is a key factor. The only way you can permanently get control is to have a good understanding of how the human machine works along with the tools necessary to intervene when you need to.

Cognitive-Behavioral Therapy

CBT is a collaborative effort between the therapist and the client. Cognitive-behavioral therapist seeks to learn what their clients want out of life (their goals) and then help their clients achieve those goals. The therapist's role is to listen, teach, and encourage, while the client's role is to speak, learn, and implement what he or she learns.

Burris MIND/FITNESS

The very first step in MIND/FITNESS is to establish an emotional baseline. After that, CBT is similar to BMF in that what the client wants is established. From there through the use of responding to statements and questions, the client literally puts their subconscious on paper. After getting to the deepest level of the subconscious, the client is able to determine what is working and what is not working for them. From there the client begins the process of restructuring the information that is driving the behavior that does not work for them.

Cognitive-Behavioral Therapy

CBT is based on stoic philosophy. Cognitive-behavioral therapy does not tell people how to feel. However, most people seeking therapy do not want to feel the way they do. CBT teaches the benefits of feeling, at worst, *calm* when confronted with undesirable situations. It also emphasizes the fact that we have our undesirable situations whether we are upset about them or not. If we are upset about our problems, we have two problems: the problem and our being upset about it. Most sane people want to have the fewest number of problems possible.

Burris MIND/FITNESS

BMF does not dictate anything to the client about how they should feel. It does, however, focus on how to take control of the emotional state at the very core of the subconscious. You will always move toward pleasure and away from pain. It is the perception of pleasure and pain that you are taught to take control of. Some things you perceive as pleasure may not be working and some things you perceive as pain may not be working. The bottom line is to have control of how you perceive everything in your life which will give you supreme control over your emotional state.

Cognitive-Behavioral Therapy

CBT uses the Socratic Method. Cognitive-behavioral therapists want to gain a very good understanding of their client's concerns. That's why they often ask *questions.* They also encourage their clients to ask questions of themselves like, "How do I really know that those people are laughing at me? Could they be laughing about something else?"

Burris MIND/FITNESS

BMF is based on a single fundamental question: What determines your emotional state and behavior? What determines your emotional state and behavior is just **information**. From this initial question you simply ask the next logical questions which are: What are the components of this **information** and how do I **Recognize, Access** and **Change** the **information** that does not work for me? This is accomplished by finding out how you communicate with yourself, especially in the form of questions. The questions you ask yourself are always going to be more important than the questions someone else asks you.

Cognitive-Behavioral Therapy

CBT is structured and directive. Cognitive-behavioral therapists have a specific agenda for each session. Specific techniques/concepts are taught during each session. CBT focuses on helping the client achieve the goals they have set. CBT is directive in that respect. However, CBT therapists do not tell their clients *what* to do; rather, they teach their clients *how*.

Burris MIND/FITNESS

BMF is a structured program process. This process is based on over 20 years of research and development. The initial foundation of BMF is based on what works and what does not work for the client. An important similarity between BMF and CBT is that it does not tell people what to do. It guides them through the process of how to get it done.

Cognitive-Behavioral Therapy

CBT is based on an educational model. CBT is based on the scientifically supported assumption that most emotional and behavioral reactions are learned. Therefore, the goal of therapy is to help clients *unlearn* their unwanted reactions and to learn a new way of reacting. While CBT therapists do not present themselves as "know-it-alls," the assumption is that if clients knew what the therapist had to teach them, the clients would not have the emotional/behavioral problems they are experiencing. Therefore, CBT has nothing to do with "just talking." People can "just talk" with anyone. The educational emphasis of CBT has an additional benefit: it leads to long-term results. When people understand **how and why** they are doing well, they can continue doing what they are doing to make themselves well.

Burris MIND/FITNESS

BMF agrees with CBT in that almost all behavior is learned, and if you have learned it, you can unlearn it and replace it with something else that works better. BMF believes that what you have learned and subconscious programming are synonymous. This is why the most fundamental issue in BMF is to take control of your subconscious programming. The question is: Do you want to control your programming or do you want your programming to control you?

Cognitive-Behavioral Therapy

CBT theory and techniques rely on the Inductive Method. A central aspect of *Rational* thinking is that it is based on *fact,* not simply our assumptions made. Often, we upset ourselves about things when, in fact, the situation isn't like we thought it was. If we had known that, we would not have wasted our time upsetting ourselves. Therefore, the inductive method encourages us to look at our thoughts as being hypotheses that can be questioned and tested. If we find that our hypotheses are incorrect (because we have new information), then we can change our thinking to be in line with how the situation really is. There are over 25 very common mental mistakes that people make that cause them to not have the facts straight.

Burris MIND/FITNESS

Integrity is a key issue when taking control of your emotional state and behavior and is one the things you must learn if you wish to stay focused and perpetuate your success. It is not what happens to you, it is how you perceive these events. This is why it is necessary to take and have control over your subconscious programming.

Cognitive-Behavioral Therapy

Homework is a central feature of CBT. If when you attempted to learn your multiplication tables you spent only one hour per week studying them, you might still be wondering what 5 X 5 equals. You very likely spent a great deal of time at home studying your multiplication tables, maybe with flashcards. The same is the case with psychotherapy. Goal achievement (if obtained) could take a very long time if all a person thought about was the techniques and topics taught for only one hour per week. That's why CBT therapists assign reading assignments and encourage their clients to practice the techniques learned.

Burris MIND/FITNESS

BMF is a set of tools that you will use anytime you wish to gain access to the deepest level of the subconscious and discover what may be sabotaging your goals. "The Heart of MIND/FITNESS" is a daily MIND/FITNESS exercise that you will use to keep yourself alert and aware of what works and does not work. It will also keep you moving in the direction that you established on the first page of the Subconscious Perspective.

The problem with all forms of psychotherapy

The problem with all forms of psychotherapy is that there is no foundational uniformity. A therapist could start with CBT and jump in with psychoanalysis. I consider CBT to be the most advanced form of psychotherapy, and if you are seeking conventional counseling, this is the one to look for. You need to ask a couple of key questions during your search. Do not ask if they use CBT, let them tell you.

1) Which form of therapy do you use? If the answer to this is CBT, then ask the next question.
2) Do you use any other forms of therapy in conjunction with CBT? If the answer to this is yes, ask which ones and then it is up to you to decide if you wish to move forward.

Why Burris MIND/FITNESS works for everyone

The reason Burris MIND/FITNESS works for everyone is that it is designed to shape itself around each individual once the foundation is established as opposed to trying to get the individual to conform to it.

Please see the Bibliography at the end of the book for recourses for this chapter.

PART TWO

7 STEPS TO TAKING CONTROL OF
YOUR SUBCONSCIOUS

5

THE EMOTIONAL CHECKLIST

In order to effectively address the behavior you want to change, you need to establish a foundation that will allow you the flexibility of dealing with the specifics of what you wish to change. This is why MIND/FITNESS works for everyone because it establishes a solid foundation from which to work.

The Burris MIND/FITNESS Full Spectrum Program is broken down into seven steps. The Full Spectrum Program is used to guide people through the process of taking control. It is called full spectrum because it covers the full range of behavior and emotions. This is absolutely necessary if you want to affect any single issue. Once you begin to peel away the layers of your behavior, you may initially think that the only behavior you have to address is your eating; but, the emotional states that may be driving it can cover the full spectrum of behavior. This is why clients often comment that this program process could be used for anything, and this is completely intentional.

If you do not want to write in the book the Emotional Checklist, the entire Full Spectrum Program and the Consultants Guidelines is available to print out on the CD. The Emotional Checklist is named EmotionalChecklist.pdf and The Burris MIND/FITNHESS Full Spectrum Program is named FullSpectrum.pdf and the Consultants Guidelines are named Guidelines.pdf. These are Adobe Acrobat files. Acrobat is a free program from Adobe that will allow this document to work on any computer. If you do not have this free program go to www.adobe.com/products/acrobat/readstep2.html.

Other reasons to print out the documents from the CD are to maintain your privacy. You will eventually need to print it out so that you can follow up on yourself and see exactly what you may want to improve on.

You cannot get control unless you start by understanding how you talk to yourself, how you feel, and what your perception of the world is. The big question when attempting to initiate any change in your life is: Where do you start? A simple answer of course would be at the beginning. The next question would be: Where is the beginning? The beginning is to find out how you feel right now on some sort of sliding scale. It is imperative that you establish a baseline and document everything; otherwise, how do you know where you started, where you are going, or where you have ended up? This was another thing I found troubling about going to a psychologist. I would sit there talking to the psychologist while he would be writing things down. I would always be thinking: "Shouldn't I be the one writing?" The answer to this was, of course, an emphatic "Yes."

The Emotional Checklist has three sections; the first section is the Emotional Checklist. This is the section that will help you understand how you are doing emotionally right now and the areas you need to give the most attention. The second is the Behavior Control Checklist. This section is designed to establish how well you understand how a behavior works and also explores the issues of food and fitness. Regardless of what you are attempting to change, food and fitness will always be key components to how you feel. The third section is the Relationship Satisfaction Scale. This is important because if you are speaking negatively to yourself, this will usually carry through to how you speak to others.

Emotional Checklist

Please place a score of 0 to 10 that indicates how you have felt in the past week.

NOT AT ALL - SOMEWHAT   –   MODERATELY - A LOT

0 ————————————— 5 ————————————— 10

Questions:

1) Have you been feeling sad or down in the dumps?	1
2) Does your future look hopeless?	0
3) Do you feel worthless or think of yourself as a failure?	1
4) Do you feel inadequate or inferior to others?	1
5) Do you get self-critical and blame yourself for everything?	3
6) Do you have trouble making up your mind?	2
7) Have you been feeling resentful or angry?	3
8) Have you lost your interest in your career, hobby, family or friends?	2

Emotional Checklist (Continued)

Please place a score of 0 to 10 that indicates how you have felt in the past week.

NOT AT ALL - SOMEWHAT   –   MODERATELY - A LOT

0 ————————————— 5 ————————————10

Questions:

9) Do you feel overwhelmed and have to push yourself hard to do things?	4
10) Do you think you look old or unattractive?	8
11) Have you lost your appetite or do you overeat or binge compulsively?	2
12) Do you suffer from insomnia or find it hard it hard to get a good night sleep? Or are you excessively tired and sleeping too much?	2
13) Have you lost interest in sex?	4
14) Do you find yourself worrying about family friends, self, future Etc?	5
15) Do you have thoughts that life is not worth living?	0
16) Do you ever have feelings of hatred toward anyone, anything, or yourself?	2

Behavior Control Checklist

Please place a score of 0 to 10 after each question that indicates your understanding of how behavior works.

NOT AT ALL - SOMEWHAT   –   MODERATELY - A LOT

0 ————————————— 5 ————————————10

Questions:

1) How would you rate your understanding of how a behavior works?	7
2) How would your rate your ability to unlearn behaviors that do not work for you?	9
3) How do you rate your ability to regulate your emotional state?	9
4) How much control do you feel you have over your thoughts?	8
5) How would you rate your confidence in achieving your goals?	9
6) How would you rate your ability to communicate effectively with yourself and other people?	8
7) How would you rate the control you have over your eating habits?	5
8) How would you rate your ability of self-motivation for exercise?	5
9) How confident do you feel in making a permanent change in your diet and exercise program?	8

Relationship Satisfaction Scale

Please place a score of 0 to 10 that indicates your degree of satisfaction.

NOT AT ALL - SOMEWHAT   –   MODERATELY - A LOT

0 ————————————— 5 —————————————10

Questions:

1) Communication and openness?	7
2) Resolving conflicts and arguments?	7
3) Degree of affection and caring?	8
4) Intimacy and closeness?	7
5) Satisfaction with your role in the relationship?	7
6) Satisfaction with your partner's role in the relationship?	7
7) Overall satisfaction with your relationship?	7

You have now established a baseline so that you not only know where you have started, but you can also begin to identify areas that need the most work.

Not all of these questions may be applicable to you. If you are a parent and want to find out how your child is doing, you will need to edit out the questions that do not apply.

What does your score mean

Before you have an accurate assessment of yourself, you need to put yourself through the Burris MIND/FITNESS Full Spectrum Program and then retest yourself without looking at the first one and see how you are doing.

The Emotional Checklist - Your objective is the lowest score possible. If any of your responses are 4 or lower, there is not a big need for concern, but I would address it and try to bring the number down. If any of your responses are a 5 or above, you definitely need to monitor this issue and make a focused assault on it. A sustained 10 on any of these issues indicates that you need to see either your physician or a psychiatrist and discuss the possibility of medication. The total score on all of these is not as important as the individual scores.

The Behavior Control Checklist - Your objective here is the highest score possible. It is important to try and score yourself accurately. If you **think** you know how a behavior works, this is a lot different than **knowing** how a behavior works. You will know how an emotional state and behavior come about after putting yourself through the program process and therefore, your score will go up.

Relationship Satisfaction Scale - Your objective here is the highest score possible. One of the key issues of the program process of MIND/FITNESS is how you speak to yourself. When you change how you speak to yourself, it is reflected when you speak to others. This will raise your score in this area as well.

After you have completed the 7 step program, you will want to do another Checklist within 24 hours, after that a minimum of once a week for one month. The length of time you stay with the program is dependent upon how significant the changes are that you need to make and of course your age and gender. The bottom line is the program process of MIND/FITNESS is how the machine works, and it will be up to you to continue to implement the tools you have learned until you get what you want.

6

STEP 2

SUBCONSCIOUS PERSPECTIVE & EMPOWERING QUESTIONS

In this section you will literally put your subconscious on paper. If you do not want to write in the book, the full document is available to print out on the CD. The document is named FullSpectrum.pdf. There will be an introduction and an instruction set for each section. This first section is simply 4 statements and one question that you need to respond to. This is all about extracting information from the subconscious.

Your Goals

The first statement you need to respond to is about your goals. Your goals are broken down into four categories and they are your Love, Health, Wealth, and Self Image.

Following each goal category will be questions that will help to generate as much information as possible about your goals. There are two key words that I want you to keep in mind while writing down your goals and they are **ABSOLUTELY MUST**. Before you write down a goal, it must be clearly defined in your mind as an **ABSOLUTELY MUST** just like you **ABSOLUTELY MUST** pay the rent or you **ABSOLUTELY MUST** eat and drink to stay alive. If you have no goals that are an **ABSOLUTELY MUST** then ask yourself the question: What objectives in my life are an **ABSOLUTELY MUST**?

Book mark the next page after you have filled it out because you are going to reference this section when you get to **Empowering Questions.**

Subconscious Perspective

Love

Please write down all the goals you **ABSOLUTELY MUST** accomplish that pertain to your love.

1) Love -
A) Listen to Matt and be there physically & emotionally no matter what mood I am in.
B) Spend more time with my Dad & call him more
C) Keep a mentally focused frame of mind when Mama talks weird to me
D) Focus on friends that have stuck around and keep in touch

Questions for Your Love Goals

- Do I need to be more respectful and loving toward my family?
- Do I need to improve my listening habits and time together?
- Do I need to become more spiritually centered and establish a greater sense of purpose and inner peace?

Subconscious Perspective

Health

Please write down all the goals you **ABSOLUTELY MUST** accomplish that pertain to your health.

1) Health -
A) Concentrate on eating healthily "Your body is a temple" - Lifestyle Change
B) Increase ability in running program by increasing distance each week
C) keep up on doctors appts
D) Lose weight & eat right & exercise in the proper mental state of mind - do not overdo!

Questions for Your Health Goals

- Do I need to lose weight, and upgrade my appearance?
- Do I need to increase my work out program and improve my nutrition?
- Do I need to increase the regularity of my medical check ups?
- Do I need to have a greater level of control over my emotional state and behavior?

Subconscious Perspective

Wealth

Please write down all the goals you **ABSOLUTELY MUST** accomplish that pertain to your wealth.

1) Wealth -
A)
B)
C)
D)

Questions for Your Wealth Goals

- Do I need to increase my job satisfaction, purpose, and confidence?
- Do I need to manage my time better?
- Do I need to fulfill the divine design of my life?

Subconscious Perspective

Self-Image

Please write down all the goals you **ABSOLUTELY MUST** accomplish that pertain to your self-image.

1) Self-Image -
A)
B)
C)
D)

Questions for Your Self-Image

- Do I need to improve my sense of humor?
- Do I need to improve my self-confidence and my ability to communicate?
- Do I need to improve my self-esteem and my self-worth?

Questions for All Your Goals

1) What other goals can I think of that **I ABSOLUTELY MUST** acquire?

2) What goals can I think of that would give me tremendous pleasure if acquired?

3) What other goals would I like to acquire, but I feel may be too difficult?

Subconscious Perspective

My Reasons

2) Please list the reasons why you feel you **ABSOLUTELY MUST** do to accomplish your goals.

A)
B)
C)
D)

Questions for Your Reasons

- How will the accomplishment of my goals affect my income?
- How will accomplishing my goals affect my personal and professional relationships?
- Will I feel more spiritually centered?
- Will I feel a greater sense of power and control over my emotional state and behavior?
- Are there medical or health reasons for accomplishing my goals?
- How will the accomplishment of these goals affect my self-confidence?

Subconscious Perspective

What I **Absolutely Must** Do

2) Please write down what you feel you **ABSOLUTELY MUST** do to accomplish your goals.

A)
B)
C)
D)

Questions for what you ABSOLUTELY MUST do to accomplish your goals.

- Do I feel I need to manage my time better?
- Do I feel I need to spend more time in meditation or prayer?
- Do I feel I need to be more honest with my family, friends, or co-workers?
- Do I feel I need a personal trainer?

Excuses

Right now excuses are the barriers that are keeping you from what you want. It is important, however, to think of as many excuses as you possibly can because you are going to find out how to use these excuses to quickly move you toward your new goals.

Subconscious Perspective

Excuses

2) Please list all of the excuses that keep you from attaining your goals.

A)
B)
C)
D)

Questions for Your Excuses

- Do I use a friend or family member as an excuse?
- Do I use your work situation or time as one of my excuses?
- Do I use any medical problems as an excuse?
- Do I use the weather or cost and distance from the health club as an excuse?
- Do I feel a lack of will power has kept me from accomplishing my goals?
- Do I use my past failures as an excuse?

A Question about Your Questions

Before you respond question 5, I need to ask you a question: Do you ask yourself questions? Yes. You ask yourself questions on an ongoing basis and those questions to yourself begin as soon as you get up each morning. You ask questions like: "What do I need to do today?" *or* "What am I going to wear?" *or* "Whom do I need to call?" *or* "Where are my keys?" With this in mind...

Subconscious Perspective

My Questions

2) Do you feel confident you can accomplish your goals, and if not, what questions do you ask about them?

A)
B)
C)
D)

A Question for Your Question

- If you do not currently ask yourself questions about your goals, what questions would you ask yourself if you did?

Why is question 5 a key component in regard to your subconscious? When I ask you a question, "What part of your consciousness usually gives you a response?" **Your subconscious**!! Now if I ask you a question about questions that you ask yourself, you have now gained access to the deepest level of the subconscious. **This is the very beginning of the process that brings about an emotional state, which in turn determines your behavior.**

Does your mind work on questions when you're not consciously involved? Yes! If you have ever asked yourself the question: What is that person's name? You may not get an answer right away, but maybe in an hour or two or maybe even the next day while you are doing something totally unrelated, the answer comes popping into your head as clear as day. Your subconscious will generate a response to absolutely every question you ask yourself even if it has to make one up.

Now that you know the mind works on questions when we are not consciously involved, how important then does the structure of the questions you ask yourself become? It becomes very important. What do you think the results of these questions will be if you are asking yourself questions like: "Why can't I maintain a consistent fitness program?" *or* "Why can't I stop eating unhealthy foods?" *or* "Why can't I accomplish my goals?" These questions will give you more excuses or keep you anchored to what you do not want.

If you have any questions written down in the Subconscious Perspective that have a don't or can't in them, these questions will be turned into **Empowering Questions** such as: "How can I keep myself on a consistent exercise program and have a good time doing it?" *or* "How can I make sure that I eat only foods that work for me?" *or* "What action do I need to take to make sure I am always moving quickly toward my goals?" If you are not happy with the results you are getting, this is one of the things you **ABSOLUTELY MUST** do consistently if you what to make a change.

Empowering Questions

After you have established your goals and how you communicate to yourself about them on the deepest level of the subconscious, you need to initiate control and implement your new programming. You will do this by turning all of your goals, statements, and questions from The Subconscious Perspective into positive **Empowering Questions**.

Most **Empowering Questions** will begin with: "How can I" *or* "What actions do I need to take to" *or* "What do I need to do to?" For example: If one of your goals is to lose 25 pounds and maintain a more consistent fitness program, an **Empowering Question** might be: "How can I permanently lose 25 pounds and have more fun with my fitness plan?"

You do not have to agonize over a question. All you have to do is to continue asking and eventually the subconscious will come up with an answer. You do need to make sure you continue coming back and ask your **Empowering Questions** until they are answered. Once all of your questions are answered, ask yourself: "Am I completely happy with this answer?"

You will start the process of **Empowering Questions** with your goals.

Your Goals

Why do you set goals? You set goals so the mind has some place to go. Do you ever get in your car and start driving without a destination? Maybe sometimes you do but even then at some point you have to establish a destination even if it is to just stop and get more gas.

You establish goals to give the mind some place to go and of course the two key words when establishing your goals is, **ABSOLUTELY MUST**. Go back and place a marker at your goal page, and we will begin the process of **Empowering Questions**.

Empowering Questions

My Love Goals

Please turn all of your responses from your **Love** goals into positive
Empowering Questions on this page.

Empowering Questions   Answers

A)	A)
B)	B)
C)	C)
D)	D)

Empowering Questions

My Health Goals

Please turn all of your responses from your **Health** goals into positive **Empowering Questions** on this page.

Empowering Questions	Answers
A)	A)
B)	B)
C)	C)
D)	D)

Empowering Questions

My Wealth Goals

Please turn all of your responses from your **Wealth** goals into positive
Empowering Questions on this page.

Empowering Questions	Answers
A)	A)
B)	B)
C)	C)
D)	D)

Empowering Questions

My Self-Image

Please turn all of your responses from your **Self-Image** goals into positive **Empowering Questions** on this page.

Empowering Questions	Answers
A)	A)
B)	B)
C)	C)
D)	D)

Your Reasons

We refer to your reasons for accomplishing your goals as anchors. Anchors are what attach you to any one particular behavior. First you give the mind somewhere to go, and then you anchor yourself to those new goals to assure that you will keep moving toward them. Excuses are also anchors, but they are keeping you attached to what you do not want.

In just one minute I'm going to show you how to use those excuses as a fast moving vehicle that will move you toward your goal instead of keeping you away from your goals which is what they are doing now. I want you to take a look at your goals and if you were unable to think of a good reason for accomplishing that goal, put a check mark next to it. This will remind you to go back until you think of a good reason for accomplishing that goal.

Empowering Questions

My Reasons

Please turn all of your responses from the **Reasons** why you feel you **ABSOLUTELY MUST** accomplish your goals into **Empowering Questions** on this page.

Empowering Questions	Answers
A)	A)
B)	B)
C)	C)
D)	D)

What You **ABSOLUTELY MUST** do

Writing down what you need to do to accomplish your goals is like making a map. You always need to clearly define what action needs to be taken in order to get from point A to point B. It is also important because you can turn that map into **Empowering Questions**, which is what you are going to do now.

Empowering Questions

What I ABSOLUTELY MUST do

Please turn all of your responses from what you feel you
ABSOLUTELY MUST do to accomplish your goals into
Empowering Questions on this page.

Empowering Questions	Answers
A)	A)
B)	B)
C)	C)
D)	D)

How to Use Excuses

As a brief reminder, your subconscious will work on and generate a response for every question you ask. If you turn your excuse into a positive **Empowering Question** and continue to repeat it as a question, the mind will no longer be able to use it as an excuse. For example, if one of your excuses is time, you can turn that excuse into a question such as: "How can I find more time to spend on my diet and exercise program and have a good time with it?" If you continue to repeat this as a question, the mind will no longer be able to use it as an excuse. What you have done is not only pulled that anchor up, but it has also become a high-speed vehicle to move you more quickly toward your goals. This is why you must write down every excuse that you can think of because you can immediately turn it into a fast moving vehicle as opposed to dead weight in regard to your goals.

Empowering Questions

Excuses

Please turn all of your excuses into **Empowering Questions** on this page.

Empowering Questions   Answers

Empowering Questions	Answers
A)	A)
B)	B)
C)	C)
D)	D)

Questions – From Negative to Positive

You now know you ask yourself questions and the subconscious works on those questions when you are not consciously involved. It is imperative that you listen to your self talk and change every negative question you ask yourself into a positive **Empowering Question**. You will begin this process by starting with the questions you asked about your goals.

Ask yourself if you will be completely happy with the results of the questions you asked in question 5 of the Subconscious Perspective. If the answer is no, restructure every one in a form that will empower you and continue to repeat it until you get what you want.

Empowering Questions

Your Questions About Your Goals

Please turn your negative self-questions from question 5 into positive **Empowering Questions** on this page.

Empowering Questions	Answers
A)	**A)**
B)	**B)**
C)	**C)**
D)	**D)**

The Five Key Questions

There are five key questions that you will be asking yourself every day:

1) Does this work for me?

2) How do I feel and will I benefit from the results of this?
   If the answer to this is no, ask yourself this next question.

3) What can I replace this with that I will benefit from?

The two key questions to use instead of reprimanding yourself are:

4) What can I learn from this?
   and
5) How can I use this experience to move myself more quickly toward my goals?

There is a detailed explanation of the importance of these key questions in chapter 9. The Heart of MIND/FITNESS

7

STEP 3

SUBCONSCIOUS SELF-IMAGE

This is Step 3 of the program process which addresses the second component of MIND/FITNESS, your subconscious pictures.

Before we get started on this one, I would like to ask you a question. Do you feel good about yourself right now? Starting right now I want you to feel fantastic about yourself on all levels because once again it is like setting a goal, only this time it is in terms of the perception you have of yourself. If you do not feel good about yourself right now, the mind has no place to go.

I am sure you have heard of the term visualization, but why is it important to visualize? It is important to visualize because it is like setting a goal, it gives your mind someplace to go. For example, if you see yourself as out of shape, insecure with your job or relationship or have a low self-image, the subconscious is going to do what ever it needs to, to keep you there. If you set a goal that has to do with a change of your physical image without restructuring the image in your subconscious, your chances of success are at best remote. It is like wearing clothes that do not fit. You can wear them, but you are never comfortable. This discomfort will lead you back to where you began.

How important is it that you establish the mental image of the person you want to be? It is imperative. It is also important to check the image you have of yourself every day to make sure you are maintaining your new self-image.

One of the primary issues for not maintaining your weight loss is because you did not restructure the image you have of yourself before you got started. Once you achieved your goal weight, the subconscious did everything it could to get you back to the image that was locked in there. This is what this chapter is all about. There will never be a more important image you have in your subconscious mind or a more important image that you will need to change than the image you have of yourself right now.

As you now know, it is essential that the image you have of yourself in your subconscious mind, must match your goal. **Writing down a detailed description of your new self-image will be the most effective way of implanting your new self-image into your subconscious.** Going back and reading the description of your new self-image as part of your daily MIND/FITNESS program will make this image a permanent part of your new subconscious programming.

Subconscious Self-Image

How You See Yourself

1) Please describe in detail how you see yourself after you have attained your goals.

Questions for Your New Self-Image

A) Do you see yourself firm and toned?

B) What is the weight or your new body?

C) What are the measurements of your chest, waist, and hips?

D) How are other people reacting to you in this picture?

It is important that you learn to associate activities that you know you will enjoy with your new self-image because becoming more active is an essential factor in attaining and maintaining a positive self-image. With this in mind let us continue.

Subconscious Self-Image

Your Activities

2) Please describe the activities you see yourself participating in after attaining your goals.

Questions for Your Activities

A) Do you see yourself doing aerobics, jogging, lifting weights, going for a brisk walk, or maybe just parking further away from the entrance while going shopping?

The subconscious will always move toward pleasure and away from pain. This is why it is crucial that your new subconscious self-image is detailed, crystal clear and you derive tremendous pleasure from it.

Subconscious Self-Image

How you feel

3) Please write down the feelings you experience from your new self-image.

| |
| |
| |
| |
| |

Questions for Your Feelings

A) Do you feel like you have become more of a magnet for everything you desire?

B) Do you feel a greater sense of spiritual strength?

C) What location could you put yourself in that would give you the most incredible feeling? Example: On vacation with someone you love, with family and friends, or maybe in a quiet place just meditating.

D) Do you feel a tremendous sense of accomplishment? Not just over yourself but the things around you as well?

Writer Producer Director

You are now the writer, producer, and director of your subconscious self-image. You can create the exact image you wish. You can participate in an activity you enjoy and in an emotional state and location that makes you feel incredible. Make your new subconscious body image as real and pleasurable as possible.

Maintenance Questions

What do you do if you have a difficult time maintaining the new image? Questions play an important role here as well. If you are having a difficult time maintaining the new perception of yourself, ask the following questions.

1) How can I maintain the image of this positive perception every second, every minute, every hour of the day?
2) What do I need to do to maintain this new image?
3) What can I add to the picture that will help me maintain this new image?
4) What do I need to do to feel fantastic all the time?
5) What action do I need to take today that will make me feel great?

Any time you run out of questions, ask yourself:

6) What questions can I ask myself that will help me maintain this new positive empowering image?

There is one more variable here, and that is, there might be something in the way of the consistent maintenance of your new pictures. If so, ask yourself the next two questions:

7) What is getting in the way of the maintenance of my new picture?
   or
8) What do I need to unlearn that will help clear up the image of my new picture?

You need to go back and reread your three responses from your Subconscious Self-Image every day because you need to have a very clear vision of how the new self appears, and most importantly, feels in mind, body, and spirit. Remember that every time you go back and reread this, you are making an assault on the old programming. It is important to continue this assault until the subconscious accepts this new picture as to how you should look and feel.

The Structure of Your Subconscious Pictures

The way you are able to determine positive from negative experiences is the way an image is stored in the subconscious or the structure of that image. Following, you will discover how you store the visual information that creates a positive emotional state for you and then use that information to help you maintain your focus and motivation toward your goals.

I think we can all agree that we are all basically wired the same, but the reason one person loses motivation and another says never quit, lie in the way each of us codes our internal pictures. In other words, every person's perception of what they are doing is different. This is why two people can experience the same event but have a totally different perception or feeling about it.

Before we begin, you need to clearly understand how to **Associate** and **Dissociate**. Right now association and dissociation happens automatically; in other words, how you feel about events in your life and yourself determine whether you associate or dissociate with the experience. If you are out of shape, over or under eat, or are abusive toward your body, you are dissociating from it. Association and dissociation must be intentional if you want a greater level of control over how you feel.

Association and dissociation is the equivalent of you watching your life's movie. If I ask you to **Dissociate** from a picture, that means that you are in the theatre looking at yourself in the picture. You may need to further dissociate from the picture if it is one that you are particularly uncomfortable with. This will mean that you will put yourself in the balcony looking down at yourself watching yourself in the picture. When I ask you to **Associate** with a picture of yourself, this simply means that you place yourself in the picture and fully become part of that experience.

You will now begin with defining the structure of a subconscious picture. Make sure you are in a quiet place where you can fully concentrate. Think about your new self-image as you detailed it in this chapter and establish all the positive associated feelings of love, health, and wealth. Do what ever you need to, to fully focus and concentrate on the formation of this picture. When you look at this picture, you feel total love and feel life could not be better. It could be a vacation, a new love or whatever you wish. You will refer to this picture as your **Motivation Picture**.

Once you have established your new image, we will explore the composition. Is the picture you see of that experience in color or black and white? If it is in black and white, turn it in to color; if it is already in color, make the colors more pleasing and vibrant. Is the picture framed, unframed, or panoramic? If the picture is framed or a certain size, make it panoramic so that it completely encompasses your field of vision.

Is the picture moving like a film or is it still? If the picture is still, add movement. If the picture is too fast or too slow, adjust the speed so that it is completely comfortable for you.

Is there sound in the form of voices, music, ambient, or nothing? If there is a voice or voices you find immensely pleasing, add them in and delete the rest; now add your favorite music or ambient sound like ocean waves, birds chirping or a gentle breeze.

Is the picture bright and clear or slightly out of focus? If the picture is out of focus, make it perfectly clear; if it is clear, make it brighter, sharper, and clearer until it is overwhelmingly pleasing. Take a few moments to structure this picture so that it is the most compelling experience you have ever had. Now, associate with this picture and place yourself in that experience. Give yourself a moment to solidly plant yourself in there. Did you feel different when you became part of this experience?

Step out of this picture and put the image aside for a moment, and we will establish what you will refer to as your **Goal Picture**. This time I want you to create a picture of yourself in a fitness program that you feel will establish the goals you established in the Subconscious Perspective.

Take a moment and be sure to get a clear image of this picture. When you have established the image, let's take a look at the composition. Is the picture in color or black and white? Is the picture framed, unframed, or panoramic? How big is the image and where is it located? Is the picture moving like a film or is it still?

If it is moving, is the speed fast, slow, or normal? Is there sound in the form of voices, ambient, or nothing? Is the picture bright and clear or slightly out of focus?

Once you have established the composition of the **Goal Picture,** I want you to bring back the motivation picture and place it in front of the **Goal Picture**. Step into the motivation picture and completely associate it. Now punch a tiny, tiny pinhole through the motivation picture so you can look through it and see the **Goal Picture**.

While looking through the pin hole, begin to change the structure of the **Goal Picture** to match the motivation picture. In other words, if the **Goal Picture** is in black and white, turn it into color. Now make it panoramic. Do the same with the sound, speed and resolution as well as any other differences you can see.

Once you have reframed your **Goal Picture,** change the image of yourself until you see exactly what you want. Pause for a moment to make sure the mind, body, and spirit of the person in this picture is exactly what you want. Be sure to establish the exact physical dimensions you want along with the purest feelings of love for the person in that picture.

Be sure you remain in the motivation picture while occasionally looking through the pinhole and seeing yourself totally in control and doing what you feel is completely necessary to accomplish your goals.

If you have trouble restructuring the **Goal Picture** to match the motivation picture, you can fuse the **Goal Picture** with the motivation picture. In other words, move the **Goal Picture** into the motivation picture until both pictures become one and you see yourself in the motivation picture going through your daily fitness plan. This technique can be used with any objective in your life that needs a little more motivation behind it.

8

STEP 4

THE STOP & REPLACE SYSTEM

This is the most powerful part of the program. The Stop and Replace System will allow you to make an assault on any subconscious programming you wish to change and make dramatic changes in your emotional state and behavior. This is accomplished by using the same process that created the program to begin with. All the elements from the first three pages of the program are used on this page to help you **Recognize**, **Access** and **Change** subconscious information that does not work for you.

As a brief reminder, in order to activate an emotional state, which in turn determines your behavior, two key components must exist:

1) You must talk to yourself, which usually begins with a question *and*
2) By asking yourself a question your subconscious mind will always give you an answer, which in turn produces a correlating picture. It is from this subconscious picture that your emotional state is determined and in turn determines your behavior.

If you have a means of intervening on these key elements, then you can make a change in the way you feel, which in turn changes your behavior.

The STOP and REPLACE System Breakdown

Please take a look at the top of the Stop and Replace breakdown on the following page. Each step will be in bold below followed by an explanation.

There are seven components to the Stop and Replace System with three parts to The Switch Pattern which is the seventh step.

The STOP and REPLACE System

Please write down one habit, behavior or emotional state that you absolutely must unlearn in the box below.

➤   You will right down what you wish to unlearn here

Reasons for NOT doing this	Empowering Questions
1) This is where you will write down your reasons.	**1)** This is where you turn your reason into an empowering question.
2)	**2)**
3)	**3)**
4)	**4)**

Answers to empowering questions:

1) This is where you write your answers to your empowering questions.
2)
3)
4)

Describe your replacement picture:———➤ Associated

This is where you will describe your new picture.

Describe your old picture: ———➤ Dissociated

This is where you will describe your old picture.

The Switch Pattern

1) CUE   When you recognize your cue you will say **STOP** to **yourself.**
2) STOP When you say STOP your old picture will be destroyed.
————————————➤ SWITCH PATTERN
3) REPLACE When you say the word **REPLACE** your subconscious mind will produce your new active body image.

Stop and Replace System Samples

Following are ten Stop and Replace System samples. If you take a look at the first one, you will notice that the **Reasons for NOT doing this** and **Empowering Questions** are filled out for you. These samples are meant to help you get started with the Stop and Replace System. You should use information from the samples only if it specifically applies to you.

The STOP and REPLACE System

Please write down one habit, behavior or emotional state that you absolutely must unlearn in the box below.

> **Fear**

Reasons for NOT doing this   Empowering Questions

Reasons for NOT doing this	Empowering Questions
1) I will not procrastinate over things I know need to be done.	**1)** How can I unlearn procrastination?
2) I will feel a greater sense of control over Everything I do.	**2)** How can I gain a greater sense of control over everything I do?
3) My decision making power will greatly improve.	**3)** How can I increase my decision making power?
4) I will be able to move more quickly toward my goals.	**4)** How can I move more quickly toward my goals?

Answers to empowering questions:

1)
2)
3)
4)

Describe your replacement picture:———→ Associated

Describe your old picture: ——→ Dissociated

The Switch Pattern

1) CUE

2) STOP

———————————————→ SWITCH PATTERN

3) REPLACE

The STOP and REPLACE System

Please write down one habit, behavior or emotional state that you absolutely must unlearn in the box below.

> **Guilt**

Reasons for NOT doing this	Empowering Questions
1) I will be able to eliminate my negative self talk.	**1)** How can I eliminate my negative self talk?
2) I will feel better emotionally.	**2)** How can I feel better all the time?
3) I will eliminate behaviors that make me feel guilty.	**3)** How can I eliminate behaviors that make me feel guilty?
4) I will be able to eliminate guilt as an excuse for over eating.	**4)** How can I eliminate guilt as an excuse for over (under) eating?

Answers to empowering questions:

1)

2)

3)

4)

Describe your replacement picture:———→ Associated

Describe your old picture: ———→ Dissociated

The Switch Pattern

1) CUE

2) STOP

                                    ———→ SWITCH PATTERN

3) REPLACE

The STOP and REPLACE System

Please write down one habit, behavior or emotional state that you absolutely must unlearn in the box below.

➢ Anger

Reasons for NOT doing this	Empowering Questions
1) I will have complete control over my to communication skills.	**1)** How can I improve my communication skills?
2) I will not be able to use anger as an excuse to over (under) eat.	**2)** How can I eliminate anger as an excuse to over (under) eat?
3) I will be more loving toward myself family and friends.	**3)** How can I be more loving toward myself family and friends?
4) I will have more fun with life.	**4)** How can I have more fun with everything I do in life?

Answers to empowering questions:

1)
2)
3)
4)

Describe your replacement picture:⟶ Associated

Describe your old picture: ⟶ Dissociated

The Switch Pattern

1) CUE

2) STOP
⟶ SWITCH PATTERN

3) REPLACE

The STOP and REPLACE System

Please write down one habit, behavior or emotional state that you absolutely must unlearn in the box below.

➢ **Negative Self Talk**

Reasons for NOT doing this	Empowering Questions
1) My self-esteem will greatly improve.	**1)** What do I need to do to upgrade my self-esteem?
2) I will feel better about everything I do.	**2)** How can I feel better about everything I do in life?
3) I will feel more confident in every aspect of my life.	**3)** How can I increase my confidence in myself?
4) I will be able to move more quickly toward my goals.	**4)** How can I move more quickly toward my goals?

Answers to empowering questions:

1)
2)
3)
4)

Describe your replacement picture: ——→ **Associated**

Describe your old picture: ——→ **Dissociated**

The Switch Pattern

1) CUE
2) STOP
———————————————→ **SWITCH PATTERN**
3) REPLACE

The STOP and REPLACE System

Please write down one habit, behavior or emotional state that you absolutely must unlearn in the box below.

➢ **Procrastination**

Reasons for NOT doing this	Empowering Questions
1) I will have more time for things I truly enjoy.	**1)** How can I find more time for the things I truly enjoy?
2) I will have more time for things I truly enjoy.	**2)** How can I manage my time more efficiently?
3) I will be much more organized.	**3)** How can I improve my organization?
4) I will eliminate the obstacles that keep me from my goals.	**4)** How can I eliminate the obstacles that keep me from my goals?

Answers to empowering questions:

1)
2)
3)
4)

Describe your replacement picture:──────→ Associated

Describe your old picture: ──────→ Dissociated

The Switch Pattern

1) CUE

2) STOP

────────────────────────────→ SWITCH PATTERN

3) REPLACE

The STOP and REPLACE System

Please write down one habit, behavior or emotional state that you absolutely must unlearn in the box below.

➢ **Over (Under) Eating**

Reasons for NOT doing this	Empowering Questions
1) I will feel more in control over every aspect of my life.	**1)** How can I gain more control over every aspect of my life?
2) I will be able to establish and maintain greater self esteem.	**2)** How can I establish and maintain greater self esteem?
3) I will have a more loving relationships.	**3)** What do I need to do to be more loving toward myself & others?
4) I will feel more comfortable in social situations.	**4)** How can I feel more comfortable in social situations?

Answers to empowering questions:

1)
2)
3)
4)

Describe your replacement picture: ⟶ **Associated**

Describe your old picture: ⟶ **Dissociated**

The Switch Pattern

1) CUE
2) STOP
⟶ **SWITCH PATTERN**
3) REPLACE

The STOP and REPLACE System

Please write down one habit, behavior or emotional state that you absolutely must unlearn in the box below.

➢ **Drugs and Alcohol**

Reasons for NOT doing this	Empowering Questions
1) I will not predispose myself to liver and heart disease.	**1)** How can I improve my overall health?
2) I will not accelerate the aging process.	**2)** What do I need to do to slow down or reverse the aging process?
3) I will always be able to drive myself home.	**3)** How can I make sure I never have to leave my car anywhere?
4) I will have a greater level of power over myself.	**4)** What action do I need to take to increase my self-power and control?

Answers to empowering questions:

1)
2)
3)
4)

Describe your replacement picture: ⟶ **Associated**

Describe your old picture: ⟶ **Dissociated**

The Switch Pattern

1) CUE

2) STOP
⟶ **SWITCH PATTERN**
3) REPLACE

The STOP and REPLACE System

Please write down one habit, behavior or emotional state that you absolutely must unlearn in the box below.

> **Smoking**

Reasons for NOT doing this	Empowering Questions
1) I will not predispose myself to lung cancer and heart disease.	**1)** How can I improve the health of my heart and lungs?
2) My breath, home and clothes will not smell like stale smoke.	**2)** How can I improve the fragrance of breath, home and clothes?
3) I will not have yellow/brown tobacco stained teeth.	**3)** What do I need to do to brighten my smile?
4) I will not continually offend people who do not smoke.	**4)** How can I improve my people skills?

Answers to empowering questions:

1)

2)

3)

4)

Describe your replacement picture: ⟶ **Associated**

Describe your old picture: ⟶ **Dissociated**

The Switch Pattern

1) CUE

2) STOP

⟶ **SWITCH PATTERN**

3) REPLACE

The STOP and REPLACE System

Please write down one habit, behavior or emotional state that you absolutely must unlearn in the box below.

> **Caffeine**

Reasons for NOT doing this	Empowering Questions
1) I will not have brown teeth and bad breath.	**1)** What do I need to do to improve the appearance of my mouth?
2) I will not predispose myself to stomach problems.	**2)** How can I improve the health of my stomach?
3) I will not send my nervous system into orbit.	**3)** What do I need to do to have more control over my nervous system?
4) I will have more patience for people I care about.	**4)** How can I be more patient with the people I care about?

Answers to empowering questions:

1)

2)

3)

4)

Describe your replacement picture:———→ Associated

Describe your old picture: ———→ Dissociated

The Switch Pattern

1) CUE

2) STOP

———————————————————→ SWITCH PATTERN

3) REPLACE

The STOP and REPLACE System

Please write down one habit, behavior or emotional state that you absolutely must unlearn in the box below.

➤ **Sugar**

Reasons for NOT doing this	Empowering Questions
1) I will not be eating calories that adds fat instead of muscle.	**1)** How can I eliminate empty calories?
2) I will not be doing constant damage to my teeth and gums.	**2)** What do I need to do to eliminate damage to my teeth and gums?
3) I will not have to suffer through the low points and mood swings.	**3)** How can I eliminate my emotional low points?
4) I will have more energy for the things I enjoy.	**4)** How can I find more energy for the things I enjoy?

Answers to empowering questions:

1)

2)

3)

4)

Describe your replacement picture: ⟶ Associated

Describe your old picture: ⟶ Dissociated

The Switch Pattern

1) CUE

2) STOP

⟶ **SWITCH PATTERN**

3) REPLACE

The Stop and Replace System

Following are the blank Stop and Replace System Sheets. You will use these sheets to make an assault on programming that does not work for you and replace it with a program of your choosing. The length of the assault on the old program has several variables and they are:

1) Age
2) Gender
3) How much physical abuse was used to reinforce your programming?

The bottom line is that this is the most powerful tool you have for taking control of your subconscious programming. You must decide on your own to what extent you wish to change and how much of an assault you wish to make on your old programming.

Fear Guilt and Anger

Fear and guilt are used on us as children to try and control our behavior. As a result, these two emotional states eventually turn into anger. This is why I start out with guiding you through the process of making a full assault on these emotional states because they are also the most limiting. What you wish to unlearn from there is up to you.

Fear, guilt, and anger are also the motivation behind a wide spectrum of behaviors that do not work. Some people think they have to have fear so they don't do things like jump off a tall building. You do not have to be afraid of heights to keep yourself from jumping off a tall building. All you need to know is what the results will be and that is usually enough. Does the emotional state of fear ever need to be more than concern? The quick answer is no. You will ultimately decide when you are comfortable with this emotional state. If it is debilitating to you in any way, you need to make an assault on it until you control it—and it does not control you.

Fear

You will begin the process of unlearning with fear. At the top of the first blank Stop and Replace System page, please write Fear in the first box with the arrow in it. If there is something specific to you such as fear of crowds, etc., write that in next to it. Fear can also include doubt, insecurity, etc. In other words, you could be insecure about accomplishing your goals, about the way you look, about your relationships. All of these pertain to Fear.

Reasons for NOT doing this and Empowering Questions

In the left column below fear, it states Reasons for NOT doing this. If you have a difficult time thinking of Reasons for not being fearful, refer to the Stop and Replace Samples. If you refer to the samples, only use the information there if it is specific to you. Remember you also refer to the reasons for doing something as anchors so what you are doing is developing better reasons for not doing what you wish to unlearn. What might the advantages be for not being fearful? Can fear keep you from getting things done? Yes. If this applies write in: "I will not procrastinate over things I know need to be done." In the right hand column you will write a correlating **Empowering Question**. If you're positive anchor was "I will not procrastinate," the **Empowering Question** would be: "How can I unlearn procrastination?"

You will need to place a book mark in the page of the Stop and Replace sheet that you are working on so that you can easily flip back from the instruction set.

The STOP and REPLACE System

Please write down one habit, behavior or emotional state that you absolutely must unlearn in the box below.

➢

Reasons for NOT doing this	Empowering Questions
1)	1)
2)	2)
3)	3)
4)	4)

Answers to empowering questions:

1)
2)
3)
4)

Describe your replacement picture: ⟶ Associated

Describe your old picture: ⟶ Dissociated

The Switch Pattern

1) CUE

2) STOP
                                        ⟶ SWITCH PATTERN
3) REPLACE

What you have now done is given yourself a reason to move away from fear and asked a question that will begin to move you in the opposite direction. Something else has also happened here.

You have also uncovered something else you want to unlearn which is, of course, procrastination. Much of the time when you are writing down **Reasons for NOT doing this,** you will uncover other things that you may want to unlearn so **always scrutinize your reasons or anchors for anything else you wish to unlearn.**

What other positive reasons or anchors might there be for not being fearful? If you do not procrastinate, you will be more productive so your next anchor might be: "I will be more productive." The **Empowering Question** would then be: "How can I increase my productivity?" If you are not spending time on fear or procrastinating, then you would have a lot more time to spend on your food and fitness plan and other things you enjoy; so the next reason for not being fearful might be: "I will have more time to spend on my food and fitness plan and other things I enjoy." The **Empowering Question** would be: "How can I find more time to spend on my food and fitness plan and other things I enjoy?" Would the elimination of fear give you more control? Yes! So the last reason for not being fearful might be: "I will have a greater sense of control over my environment and myself." The **Empowering Question** would be: "How can I gain a greater level of control over my environment and myself?"

Answers to Empowering Questions

Right below the anchors and **Empowering Questions,** you will see a space for Answers to **Empowering Questions**. Be sure to fill this in when the answers come to you. Remember you do not have to sit and work on a question. Just keep asking and the mind will eventually give you one. It is important to come back to this every day and continue asking these questions until you are completely happy with the answers.

Describe your Replacement Picture - Associated

Describe your Replacement Picture. The most important question to ask yourself when unlearning a behavior is: What can I use to replace this habit, behavior, or emotional state with that will benefit me? You cannot just quit something and leave a blank spot in the mind; you must replace it with something before you quit. A good example of this is someone who says: "I can't quit smoking I'll gain weight." You gain weight because you did not make a conscious choice of what you were going to replace the habit with so the mind made a choice for you.

There are no limits for this replacement picture. You do however want to make the replacement picture as compelling as possible which means that you want to focus on the results as opposed to the process. In other words, everyone likes the results of exercise but very few people enjoy the process so it is important to create an image that is the most compelling to you. The basis for this new picture needs to be a combination of the results of the goals you listed in Step 2 the Subconscious Perspective and the description of the new self you wrote down in Step 2 the Subconscious Self-Image. After establishing the picture of the new self, enhance it in any way that you possibly can. For instance, add music to it if you have a favorite song, add whatever colors you want, or put people in the picture who make you feel good. Also, make sure that you always focus on the results of your replacement picture.

Example: If fear is preventing you from getting something done, you want to establish a picture of having the task done as opposed to going through the process.

Describe your Old Picture - Dissociated

Now write down a description of the old picture and remember to stay dissociated from this picture. Do you remember how to dissociate from your negative pictures? If not, go back to Step 3 and review "The Structure of Your Subconscious Pictures." **It is important that you remain dissociated from all pictures in your subconscious you wish to change.**

Your Cue for Fear

After you've written down what the old picture looks like, I want you to take a look at that picture and then back it up. That's right! Go in reverse until right before you begin the behavior. This is known as your Cue. Your Cue is also referred to as a trigger.

The Cue is the most difficult part of the Stop and Replace System sheet so if you cannot think of your Cue right now, do not concern yourself with it; just ask yourself the question: What is the Cue or trigger for this issue? It is important to recognize the Cue, so as soon as you think of it, write it down. There is always a beginning to every subconscious process, and it is imperative that you stop it before it gains power and takes over what you truly want.

The Switch Pattern for Fear

Now for the fun part, are you ready? We are going to learn how to do the switch pattern. First I would like you to get a good clear vision of your Replacement Picture, **Associated**. Do you have a clear vision of your new picture? Once you have established that picture, set it aside for a moment. Now bring up your Old Picture, **Dissociated**. Remember anytime we talk about the old picture make sure you remain dissociated from it by putting yourself in the back row of a theatre as opposed to actually being part of the picture.

When you recognize the Cue in the old picture, say **STOP** to yourself and then move the picture closer to you, make it smaller, smaller, darker and darker until it's a little black BB right in front of your face. Now shoot it back behind you and blow it up into a million molecules while saying **REPLACE** to yourself which will simultaneously bring up the new picture. That is the Switch Pattern. This is how you make a full assault on a behavior that does not work for you and create a positive permanent change in the subconscious. All the elements that constitute an emotional state and behavior are within the Stop and Replace System so as long as you maintain the assault, you will take control of your subconscious programming.

Guilt

At the top of the next Stop and Replace System page write in Guilt. If there is something specific to you such as guilt from food, not exercising, procrastination etc., write that in next to it.

Reasons for NOT doing this and Empowering Questions

In the left column below guilt it states Reasons for NOT doing this. What might the advantages be for not being guilty? If you have a difficult time thinking of advantages for not being guilty, refer to The Stop and Replace samples. Remember, when you refer to a sample, only use the information there if it is specific to you. Now what might a big advantage be for unlearning guilt? What does guilt do to you? Guilt tends to help generate your negative self-talk. Unlearning guilt will help you eliminate your negative self- talk. The reason or anchor then for not being guilty would be: "I will be able to eliminate my negative self-talk." If this is relative to you, write it down. An **Empowering Question** for this reason might be: "What do I need to do to permanently eliminate my negative self-talk?" You have also once again uncovered something you want to unlearn if you marked in eliminating negative self-talk as one of your reasons or anchors.

What other reasons or anchors are there for not being guilty? If you unlearn guilt, will you feel better emotionally? Yes. So another reason for not being guilty is: "I will feel better emotionally." A suggestion for the correlating **Empowering Question** would be: "What action do I need to take to improve my emotional state every day?"

The STOP and REPLACE System

Please write down one habit, behavior or emotional state that you absolutely must unlearn in the box below.

> ➤

Reasons for NOT doing this   Empowering Questions

Reasons for NOT doing this	Empowering Questions
1)	1)
2)	2)
3)	3)
4)	4)

Answers to empowering questions:

1)
2)
3)
4)

Describe your replacement picture:———→ Associated

Describe your old picture: ———→ Dissociated

The Switch Pattern

1) CUE
2) STOP
————————————————→ SWITCH PATTERN
3) REPLACE

Another reason for not feeling guilt is: "I will eliminate behaviors that make me feel guilty." The **Empowering Question** would be: "How can I permanently Stop behaviors that make me feel guilty."

Another reason for not being guilty is: "I will be able to eliminate guilt as an excuse for over eating, not exercising etc." The **Empowering Question** would be: "How can I permanently eliminate guilt as an excuse for over or under eating and skipping my fitness plan?"

Answers to Empowering Questions

Be sure to fill this in your Answers to **Empowering Questions** when the answers come to you. Drop down to your replacement picture.

Describe your Replacement Picture - Associated

Once again the basis for this new picture needs to be a combination of the results of the goals you listed in the Subconscious Perspective and the description of the new self you wrote down in the Subconscious Self-Image. After establishing the picture of the new self, make sure the structure is the same as your initial replacement picture and enhance it in any way that you possibly can. For instance, add music to it if you have a favorite song, add whatever colors you want, or put people in the picture who make you feel good.

Also, make sure you always focus on the results of your replacement picture. Always go for the results of not feeling guilty and **Associate** with this picture.

Describe your Old Picture - Dissociated

Make sure you keep yourself out in the audience of the theater when viewing this picture or up in the balcony looking down at yourself, looking at this picture.

Your Cue for Guilt

When you are done describing the old picture, continue to look at it and then run it backwards until right before you begin the behavior. This is your cue.

The Switch Pattern for Guilt

Are you ready for the switch pattern? First get a good clear vision of the new picture and make sure you are a part of it. Once you have established that picture, I want you to move it aside for a moment. Now establish a dissociated vision of the old picture.

When you recognize the cue in the old picture say **STOP** to yourself and then move the picture closer to you, make it smaller, smaller, darker, and darker until it's a little black BB right in front of your face.

Now shoot it back behind you and blow it up into a million molecules while saying to yourself **REPLACE** which simultaneously brings up the new picture.

Anger

In the box at the top of the next Stop and Replace System page, please write in anger. If there is something specific, add that in. In other words if you have anger toward yourself, a family member, a friend, your boss or the way your life is going.

Reasons for NOT doing this and Empowering Questions

What is one of the biggest reasons for not being angry? What is usually significantly impaired when you get angry? Do you begin to communicate differently? Yes. Your first reason for not being angry might be: "I will not lose control of my ability to communicate effectively." And of course the **Empowering Question** would be: "How can I improve my communication skills?"

What other benefits might there be for not being angry? Do you ever stuff this emotion with food? If the answer is yes, then your next reason for not doing this might be: "I will not be able to use anger as an excuse to over or under eat." The **Empowering Question** would be: "How can I eliminate anger as an excuse to over or under eat."

Would you be more loving toward yourself, your family, and others? Yes. If this pertains to you, please write it down. The **Empowering Question** for this reason would be: "How can I be more loving toward my family, others, and myself?" A suggestion for the correlating **Empowering Question** would be: "What action do I need to take to improve my emotional state every day?"

The STOP and REPLACE System

Please write down one habit, behavior or emotional state that you absolutely must unlearn in the box below.

➤

Reasons for NOT doing this   **Empowering Questions**

1)	1)
2)	2)
3)	3)
4)	4)

Answers to empowering questions:

1)
2)
3)
4)

Describe your replacement picture: ⟶ **Associated**

Describe your old picture: ⟶ **Dissociated**

The Switch Pattern

1) CUE
2) STOP
⟶ SWITCH PATTERN
3) REPLACE

Would you have more fun with life? Definitely! If this pertains to you, another reason might be: "I will have more fun with life." The **Empowering Question** would be: "How can I have more fun with everything I do in life?"

Answers to Empowering Questions

Be sure to fill this in your Answers to **Empowering Questions** when the answers come to you.

Describe your Replacement Picture - Associated

When you have finished the positive anchors and **Empowering Questions,** go to the bottom of the page and describe the new picture associated. Once again, the basis for your new picture needs to be a combination of the results of the goals you listed in Step 2 your Subconscious Perspective and the description of the new self you wrote down in Step 3 your Subconscious Self-Image.

After establishing the picture of the new self, make sure the structure is the same as your initial replacement picture and enhance it in any way that you possibly can. For instance, add music to it if you have a favorite song, add whatever colors you want, or put people in the picture who make you feel good. Also, make sure that you always focus on the results of whatever your replacement picture is.

Describe your Old Picture - Dissociated

When you have finished describing the new picture describe the old picture, dissociated.

Your Cue for Anger

Were you able to recognize your cue? If you were not able to clearly recognize your cue, just ask yourself the question: What is the cue for this picture?

The Switch Pattern for Anger

Get a clear vision of the new picture and make sure you are a part of it. Once you have established that picture, move it aside for a moment. Now establish a dissociated vision of the old picture.

When you recognize the cue in the old picture say **STOP** to yourself and then move the picture closer to you, make it smaller, smaller, darker, and darker until it's a little black BB right in front of your face. Now shoot it back behind you and blow it up into a million molecules while saying **REPLACE** to yourself which simultaneously brings up the new picture.

You will want to carefully read every STOP and REPLACE page every day to make sure every habit, behavior or emotion has been changed to your satisfaction.

If you have not begun to see significant results after 7 days, you will need to use another blank Stop and Replace sheet and rewrite all of your reasons, **Empowering Questions**, new and old picture and of course a clear identification of your Cue. Every time you reread your Stop and Replace sheet, you are making an assault on the old subconscious programming.

The bottom line is that this is how you learned what does not work; and this is how you are going to unlearn it and replace it with something that works better.

You have 7 more blank Stop and Replace pages to take control of whatever may be controlling you that does not work. It is now up to you to determine what you are happy with and what you are not happy with.

The STOP and REPLACE System

Please write down one habit, behavior or emotional state that you absolutely must unlearn in the box below.

> ➤

Reasons for NOT doing this	Empowering Questions
1)	1)
2)	2)
3)	3)
4)	4)

Answers to empowering questions:

1)
2)
3)
4)

Describe your replacement picture: ──→ Associated

Describe your old picture: ──→ Dissociated

The Switch Pattern

1) CUE
2) STOP
──────────────→ SWITCH PATTERN
3) REPLACE

The STOP and REPLACE System

Please write down one habit, behavior or emotional state that you absolutely must unlearn in the box below.

> ➤

Reasons for NOT doing this	Empowering Questions
1)	1)
2)	2)
3)	3)
4)	4)

Answers to empowering questions:

1)
2)
3)
4)

Describe your replacement picture: ⟶ **Associated**

Describe your old picture: ⟶ **Dissociated**

The Switch Pattern

1) CUE
2) STOP
⟶ SWITCH PATTERN
3) REPLACE

The STOP and REPLACE System

Please write down one habit, behavior or emotional state that you absolutely must unlearn in the box below.

> ➢

Reasons for NOT doing this   Empowering Questions

Reasons for NOT doing this	Empowering Questions
1)	1)
2)	2)
3)	3)
4)	4)

Answers to empowering questions:

1)
2)
3)
4)

Describe your replacement picture:———→ Associated

Describe your old picture: ———→ Dissociated

The Switch Pattern

1) CUE
2) STOP
———————————————→ SWITCH PATTERN
3) REPLACE

The STOP and REPLACE System

Please write down one habit, behavior or emotional state that you absolutely must unlearn in the box below.

➢

Reasons for NOT doing this   Empowering Questions

1)	1)
2)	2)
3)	3)
4)	4)

Answers to empowering questions:

1)
2)
3)
4)

Describe your replacement picture:————→ Associated

Describe your old picture: ————→ Dissociated

The Switch Pattern

1) CUE

2) STOP

————————————————→ SWITCH PATTERN

3) REPLACE

The STOP and REPLACE System

Please write down one habit, behavior or emotional state that you
absolutely must unlearn in the box below.

➢

Reasons for NOT doing this   Empowering Questions

1)	1)
2)	2)
3)	3)
4)	4)

Answers to empowering questions:

1)
2)
3)
4)

Describe your replacement picture:———→ Associated

Describe your old picture: ———→ Dissociated

The Switch Pattern

1) CUE
2) STOP
————————————————————→ SWITCH PATTERN
3) REPLACE

The STOP and REPLACE System

Please write down one habit, behavior or emotional state that you absolutely must unlearn in the box below.

> ➤

Reasons for NOT doing this   Empowering Questions

Reasons for NOT doing this	Empowering Questions
1)	1)
2)	2)
3)	3)
4)	4)

Answers to empowering questions:

1)
2)
3)
4)

Describe your replacement picture:⟶ Associated

Describe your old picture: ⟶ Dissociated

The Switch Pattern

1) CUE
2) STOP
⟶ SWITCH PATTERN
3) REPLACE

The STOP and REPLACE System

Please write down one habit, behavior or emotional state that you absolutely must unlearn in the box below.

> ➢

Reasons for NOT doing this	Empowering Questions
1)	1)
2)	2)
3)	3)
4)	4)

Answers to empowering questions:

1)
2)
3)
4)

Describe your replacement picture:——→ Associated

Describe your old picture: ——→ Dissociated

The Switch Pattern

1) CUE
2) STOP
————————————————→ SWITCH PATTERN
3) REPLACE

The most dramatic results you will ever achieve for something you wish to change will be made with the use of the Stop and Replace System. The Stop and Replace System will allow you to take control anytime you choose to do so. You are no longer subject to what you have learned or how you have been programmed. You can now ultimately decide what information remains in the subconscious and what information will not. The only question in regard to using the Stop and Replace system regularly is: "Do I want my programming to control me or do I want to take control of my programming?"

9

THE HEART OF
MIND/FITNESS

The Heart of MIND/FITNESS consists of your **Love, Health, Wealth, and Self Image.** Now that you understand how to take control of your emotional state and behavior, it is necessary that you use these skills on a daily basis. The way you process information can be dramatically changed in a short period of time, simply by consistently implementing The Heart of MIND/FITNESS.

Feel free to bend, shape, rearrange, and change any and all questions to suit your exact needs. **It is imperative that you ask yourself a minimum of one question per category every night before you go to bed and every morning after you get up.** This is the least you must do in order to maintain your minimum MIND/FITNESS.

The Five Key Questions

The First Three Key Questions You Will Ask Yourself About Everything Through the Course of Your Day Are:

1) Does this work for me?
2) How do I feel and will I benefit from the **results** of this? (If the answer is no, ask yourself this next question.)
3) What can I replace this with that I will benefit from?

The Two Key Questions to Use Instead of Reprimanding Yourself Are:

4) What can I learn from this?
    and
5) How can I use this experience to move myself more quickly toward my goals?

The first of these five questions is the most important because you can plug a lot of different things into it. For instance: Does this **program** work for me? I want you to ask yourself this question because my objective is to insure your success. You now have the resources to do that, but you need to know what is working and what does not.

Other things that you may want to plug into this first key question are: Does this food plan work for me? Does this fitness plan work for me? Does this relationship work for me? The second question is important because there are things in your life that you think may work for you, but you may not benefit from the results. The best example of this is cigarette smokers. If I ask a smoker: "Does smoking work for you?" The image they will usually see initially is kicking back, relaxing, and enjoying their cigarette so the initial answer is many times yes. If I then ask, "How do you feel and will you benefit from the results of smoking?" This brings up a totally different picture especially if you ask them to look at the results 10, 20 or 30 years from now.

You now see someone whose mouth looks like a puckered rectum, breathing has become difficult, and who has significantly shortened their quality of life. The third question is important because you can not leave a blank spot in the mind. If you do not make a choice for replacement of an emotion, habit or behavior, the mind will make one for you. The whole point of this program process is not to become who you are by accident, especially if it simply does not work.

Reprimanding yourself will not only keep you where you are but will also increase the weight of the anchor for what you do not want. Asking the last two questions will allow you to not only move away from making yourself feel bad, it will also allow you to use every experience in your life. **Nothing** in life is negative or useless if you fully understand how to speak to yourself about it.

Empowering Questions for My

Love

1) **How can I make sure I continually and perpetually live in the light of love?**

2) **What do I need to do to be more loving toward my family, others, and myself?**

3) **What do I need to unlearn that is be keeping me from my perfect love?**

4) **What action do I need to take to ensure that I perpetually live in the light of love?**

5) **What questions do I need to ask myself to ensure that I live in the light of love?**

Empowering Questions for My

Love

6) What questions do I need to ask myself during prayer, meditation, or self-hypnosis?

```



```

7) How can I be more of a magnet for my perfect love?

```



```

8) What do I need to do to perceive all relationships as beneficial?

```



```

9) How can I stay focused on being grateful for what I have been blessed with?

```



```

10) How can I make every person a golden link in the chain of my good?

```



```

Empowering Questions for My

Love

11) What do I need to do to improve all my relationships?

12) How can I make sure my love never turns to hate or fear?

13) How can I be more receptive to all the love that surrounds me every day?

14) What do I need to do to perpetuate my perfect love?

15) What questions can I ask myself that will make me more of a magnet for my perfect love?

Empowering Questions for My

Love

16) How can I improve my communication skills with the ones I love?

17) What am I willing to do to ensure my perfect love?

18) What action do I need to take to become more of a magnet for my perfect love?

19) What will happen today that will give me incredible pleasure for no reason?

20) How can I use every emotion and every life experience to move myself forward?

Empowering Questions for My

Love

21) What questions can I add to this list that will perpetually move me toward a powerful, empowering Love?

22)

23)

24)

25)

Empowering Questions for My

Health

1) **What action can I take to create positive change in my life every day?**

---

2) **How can I make sure I stay in the habit of unlearning things that do not work?**

---

3) **What do I need to do to maintain my excitement and enthusiasm for my fitness program everyday?**

---

4) **Why do I feel so excited and enthusiastic about my fitness program?**

---

5) **How can I have more fun with my new eating, exercise and other new habits?**

Empowering Questions for My

Health

6) Who or what do I need to process out my life that is keeping
   me from my perfect health?

```
_____
_____
_____
```

7) How can I use all the things in my life to move me toward my
   perfect health?

```
_____
_____
_____
```

8) How can I make sure I only ask questions that work for me
   and move me quickly toward my food and fitness goals?

```
_____
_____
_____
```

9) What exercise do I enjoy enough to make it a permanent part
   of my weekly or daily workout routine?

```
_____
_____
_____
```

10) Why do I love working out so much?

```
_____
_____
_____
```

Empowering Questions for My

Health

11) **What do I need to do to establish a permanent subconscious program that will continually move me toward my perfect health?**

12) **What do I need to do to keep my emotional state from becoming erratic?**

13) **What am I the most excited about in my life?**

14) **What do I need to do to empower myself every day?**

15) **How can I make sure I only ask questions that will propel me toward my goals?**

Empowering Questions for My

Health

16) What do I need to do to maintain a consistent exercise program?

17) What do I need to do to maintain my perfect health?

18) What is keeping me from my perfect health and what do I need to do to unlearn it or remove it from my life?

19) What questions do I need to ask myself every day to insure that I am continually moving toward my perfect health?

20) What foods will have the most positive affect on my emotional state?

Empowering Questions for My

Health

21) What questions can I add to this list that will perpetually move me toward my perfect Health?

22)

23)

24)

25)

Empowering Questions for My

Wealth

1) **What do I need to do to perceive every experience as a positive?**

_____
_____
_____

2) **How can I maximize my productivity everyday?**

_____
_____
_____

3) **What do I need to unlearn that may be keeping me form my perfect wealth?**

_____
_____
_____

4) **What do I need to do to more clearly define my goals?**

_____
_____
_____

5) **What do I need to do to maintain the focus of my goals?**

_____
_____
_____

Empowering Questions for My

Wealth

6) **What subconscious programs do I need to change to move more quickly toward my goals?**

7) **What action do I need to take to use every life experience as a stepping stone toward my goals?**

8) **What do I need to do to draw all things into my experience that will ensure my success?**

9) **How can I make sure I stay focused on the task at hand?**

10) **How can I eliminate confusion?**

Empowering Questions for My

Wealth

11) How can I keep myself up, on, centered, and focused?

12) What do I need to do to become more of a magnet for my perfect wealth?

13) How can I increase my decision-making speed?

14) What do I need to do to perpetuate my perfect wealth?

15) What am I willing to do to ensure my perfect wealth?

Empowering Questions for My

Wealth

16) How can I make sure I exploit my potential to the maximum everyday?

17) What questions do I need to ask myself to clearly define the divine design of my life?

18) How can I make all things in my life work for me?

19) How can I use all events in my life as a stepping-stone to move me toward my goals?

20) What questions do I need to ask myself everyday to ensure I am always moving in the direction of my goals?

Empowering Questions for My

Wealth

21) What questions can I add to this list that will perpetually move me toward my perfect Wealth?

22)

23)

24)

25)

Empowering Questions for My

Self-Image

1) How can I make sure I continually maintain a positive self-image?

2) What do I need to do to improve my sense of humor?

3) What do I need to do, to consistently maintain my new self-image?

4) Why am I so happy?

5) What subconscious pictures or self-talk do I need to change to insure a positive self image?

Empowering Questions for My

Self-Image

6) How can I take greater control of my emotional state?

```
_____
_____
_____
```

7) How can I make sure I fully enjoy every day of my life?

```
_____
_____
_____
```

8) What goals do I need to set in order to ensure my happiness
    and maintain a powerful self-image?

```
_____
_____
_____
```

9) What do I need to do to make sure that all levels of
    consciousness are continually and perpetually integrated?

```
_____
_____
_____
```

10) What do I need to do to maintain my emotional health?

```
_____
_____
_____
```

Empowering Questions for My

Self-Image

11) What action do I need to take everyday to maintain my emotional health?

12) What do I need to do to stay focused on all the positive aspects of my life?

13) What is the divine design of my life?

14) What do I need to do to fulfill the divine design of my life?

15) What do I need to do to make this a perfect day?

Empowering Questions for My

Self-Image

16) How can I make this the best day I've ever had?

17) What do I need to unlearn that is be keeping me from my most powerful self-image?

18) What am I willing to do to maintain my new self-image?

19) What do I need to do to perpetuate my new self-image?

20) What do I need to do to be closer to who I am instead of what I've learned?

Empowering Questions for My

Self-Image

21) What questions can I add to this list that will help me maintain my new Self-Image of Love, Health, and Wealth?

22)

23)

24)

25)

FOOD & FITNESS PLANNER

Getting consistent control of your emotional state includes consistent control of what you eat, drink, and the type and amount of exercise you get. Why is it important to plan your food and fitness schedule? It is important because the process of an unconscious assault on the body with food, alcohol, or drugs can start a day or even days before you indulge in a behavior that will throw you completely off course and out of control. Planning your food and fitness schedule is a big part of reprogramming these behaviors, and you need to plan them out until it becomes automatic.

Starting from the top you have a start date and then the week is divided into every other day. This is split up so that if you are just starting it does not become overwhelming to try and plan a food and fitness schedule every day. You always want to plan your food and fitness schedule the day before so on this first page you start on Sunday and plan your food schedule for Monday.

If you choose, you can plan your food schedule every other day and your fitness schedule every other day; or if you are feeling enthusiastic, you can plan both your food and fitness plan every day prior to the day of implementation.

Food & Fitness Plan Instruction Set

Food Plan - Please plan and schedule your meals the day before.
Emotionally Driven Food - This is where you mark in your emotionally driven food or drink. Identify the emotion and use The **STOP** and **REPLACE** System to initiate change and take control.
Fitness Plan - Please mark down the type of workout and amount of time. After you have completed your **Fitness Plan,** mark down your approximate heart rate.
Weight - A recent study has found that one of the things that people who were most successful at maintaining a consistent weight was that they weighed themselves every day. You must ultimately determine if this is going to work for you.

You have enough Food and Fitness Planner sheets for 30 days. You can of course make more copies from the CD.

Food and Fitness Planner

Start Date_____

Monday	Wednesday	Friday
Food Plan	**Food Plan**	**Food Plan**
Morning:	Morning:	Morning:
Afternoon:	Afternoon:	Afternoon:
Emotionally Driven Food	**Emotionally Driven Food**	**Emotionally Driven Food**
Fitness Plan	**Fitness Plan**	**Fitness Plan**
Weight:	Weight:	Weight:

Food and Fitness Planner

Start Date_____

Tuesday	Thursday	Saturday
Food Plan	Food Plan	Food Plan
Morning:	Morning:	Morning:
Afternoon:	Afternoon:	Afternoon:
Emotionally Driven Food	Emotionally Driven Food	Emotionally Driven Food
Fitness Plan	Fitness Plan	Fitness Plan
Weight:	Weight:	Weight:

Food and Fitness Planner

Start Date_____

Monday	Wednesday	Friday
Food Plan	**Food Plan**	**Food Plan**
Morning:	Morning:	Morning:
Afternoon:	Afternoon:	Afternoon:
Emotionally Driven Food	**Emotionally Driven Food**	**Emotionally Driven Food**
Fitness Plan	**Fitness Plan**	**Fitness Plan**
Weight:	Weight:	Weight:

Food and Fitness Planner

Start Date_____

Tuesday	Thursday	Saturday
Food Plan	Food Plan	Food Plan
Morning:	Morning:	Morning:
Afternoon:	Afternoon:	Afternoon:
Emotionally Driven Food	Emotionally Driven Food	Emotionally Driven Food
Fitness Plan	Fitness Plan	Fitness Plan
Weight:	Weight:	Weight:

Food and Fitness Planner

Start Date_____

Monday	Wednesday	Friday
Food Plan	**Food Plan**	**Food Plan**
Morning:	Morning:	Morning:
Afternoon:	Afternoon:	Afternoon:
Emotionally Driven Food	**Emotionally Driven Food**	**Emotionally Driven Food**
Fitness Plan	**Fitness Plan**	**Fitness Plan**
Weight:	**Weight:**	**Weight:**

Food and Fitness Planner

Start Date_____

Tuesday Food Plan	Thursday Food Plan	Saturday Food Plan
Morning:	Morning:	Morning:
Afternoon:	Afternoon:	Afternoon:
Emotionally Driven Food	Emotionally Driven Food	Emotionally Driven Food
Fitness Plan	Fitness Plan	Fitness Plan
Weight:	Weight:	Weight:

Food and Fitness Planner

Start Date_____

Monday	Wednesday	Friday
Food Plan	Food Plan	Food Plan
Morning:	Morning:	Morning:
Afternoon:	Afternoon:	Afternoon:
Emotionally Driven Food	Emotionally Driven Food	Emotionally Driven Food
Fitness Plan	Fitness Plan	Fitness Plan
Weight:	Weight:	Weight:

Food and Fitness Planner

Start Date_____

Tuesday	Thursday	Saturday
Food Plan	Food Plan	Food Plan
Morning:	Morning:	Morning:
Afternoon:	Afternoon:	Afternoon:
Emotionally Driven Food	Emotionally Driven Food	Emotionally Driven Food
Fitness Plan	Fitness Plan	Fitness Plan
Weight:	Weight:	Weight:

STEP 7

THE TRANCE-FORMATION

The Audio/Data CD

The CD contains both audio and data. I will explain the audio portion first. There are two tracks. Track One is an explanation of the Trance-Formation and Track Two is The Trance-Formation. Following is an explanation and the intent of the seventh and final step of the Burris MIND/FITNESS Full Spectrum Program.

The Trance-Formation

The term Trance is used to describe a subconscious state, or what you may refer to as meditation or prayer. It is a means of having a greater level of communication with the subconscious. The last half of this term, Formation, refers to the formation of information during your Trance or the structure of your self-talk and pictures. I also refer to the Trance-Formation as accelerated unlearning.

The most powerful means of changing your subconscious programming is through the use of light trance. Light trance is termed light trance because it is not intended for me to take over your subconscious. The intention is for **you** to take control of your subconscious. I am simply the facilitator. The Trance-Formation is also important because it is in essence prayer or meditation with a purpose. It is designed to help you learn how to meditate and for those who already meditate to substantially increase the power of your meditation or prayer.

During your light trance you remain aware of everything around you and in complete control. Instead of being given generic or general information, the information used during your Trance will be specific to you as established in the first six steps of the program. The purpose of the Trance-Formation is not to quiet the mind as in most forms of meditation. The mind has a certain speed it is going to run regardless of what you attempt because this is just part of being alive. You can however take control of what it is doing, and this is what the Trance-Formation is all about.

What you say to yourself is more important than anything anyone will ever say to you or about you. Once you have learned the dialogue of the induction, you can use this to put yourself in a relaxed state that will allow you greater control over your subconscious processes. It is important that you put yourself in a Light Trance at least once a day.

The effectiveness of your meditation will always be determined by what you say to yourself and the pictures you choose. The Trance-Formation requires that you are not involved in any activity. It is important before listening to the Trance-Formation that you choose a quiet place where you can relax and fully absorb this wonderful experience.

The Data on the CD

There are three PDF files and a *Read Me* first text document on the CD. In case you are not familiar with a PDF file, this is an Adobe Acrobat file that is compatible with any computer. If you do not have a reader you can go to www.Adobe.com and download a free reader.

The first PDF is "The Emotional Checklist" (Step 1 chapter 5). The second PDF is the Burris MIND/FITNESS Full Spectrum Program (Step 2 through 6 - Chapter 6 through 11). This is an important document because if you want to help someone with an eating or other behavior disorder or you need to put yourself through the program again, you will need to print this document out. The Full Spectrum Program includes a cover which can be slid into the clear front of a one half inch three ring binder. You will also need a 5 tab set to properly organize the contents.

The Table of Contents goes into the notebook first before the first tab. One important note is that the three ring punch of the first page of the Subconscious Perspective needs to be placed on the opposite side of the sheet so that it faces page 2 **Empowering Questions**. This makes it a lot easier to transfer your responses from **The Subconscious Perspective** to **Empowering Questions**.

The third PDF file is "The Consultants Guidelines." This is the guidelines that I use to do a group or one on one consultation. The Consultants Guidelines are written in script form so that anyone who chooses to use them can learn it just as you would any other script and help your child or a friend or lead a group or class. I recommend a flexible clear-front coil binding with an 8 tab set for The Consultants Guidelines. This is one tab for each step of the program and one tab for the follow up section. You can have the coil binding done at any office supply with a print section.

Maintaining Your Fit Mind

The question in regard to this program process is how long will it take to change an unwanted behavior? When I do the entire program in a single session it takes approximately 4 hours. The **Consultants Guidelines** are set up to split that into two sessions of two hours if you need to. Either way this establishes the foundation for the program and **immediately generates dramatic results** that are unseen in any other form of behavior change.

The big issue is maintenance after you have established your initial results or length of time to completely reprogram yourself. There are several variables whether an unwanted behavior will, if ever, come back. Age, gender, the amount of physical abuse, and how the behavior was learned to begin with are all factors. Let's start with age. Once past the age of 40, a behavior is going to be more difficult to unlearn and to maintain. Women seem to have about 10 to 15 years longer than men in regard to their ability to unlearn in a short period of time. In other words, men get stuck in a behavior at a much more dramatic level at a younger age. The success rate goes down for men over the age of 50 and for women over the age of 60. The recommendation for these demographics is a 30 day in-house program and possibly more with a monthly follow up for three to six months. This is not to say that you can not take control of your subconscious programming at any age, you just have to be prepared to work a lot harder on it than someone in their teens, twenties, or thirties. The last variable is how you learned the behavior. If there was physical abuse in conjunction with emotional and verbal abuse, this is going to require a greater level of maintenance at any age.

When I compiled the first version of this program process and put myself through it, the results were so dramatic that I thought I had completely fixed myself. The reality was after a few months went by, I had just peeled away a couple of surface layers so that I could make an assault on the true core issues. During the first couple of years, I ran myself through the program about four times per year. I now put myself through it twice a year. It is a wonderful thing to stay tuned up and in control. You can only move forward if your thinking remains flexible, and you become more inflexible as you age. If you understand and accept this it will make the process of change easier.

It is imperative that you follow up on yourself for a minimum of thirty days. After that you will need to determine for yourself whether or not you are satisfied with your programming and if not, you need to continue the assault.

The Emotional Checklist

The Emotional Checklist needs to be saved to your hard drive in a folder named Emotional Checklist, with the date that you filled it out as the document name (05/24/04.pdf). This will give you a baseline reference that you can refer back to. The Emotional Checklist is a form that you can type directly into with your score calculated at the bottom. The Relationship Satisfaction Scale correlates with everything else so your numbers here should also continue to improve as well unless you are with someone who insists on staying broken. This is the reason for the primary MIND/FITNESS question. Does this work for me? You fill in the blank.

Your maintenance schedule for the Emotional Checklist after the first thirty days needs to be once a month and compare it to the one you filled out the previous month. An important thing to remember is that you can always do more. The only question is how far do you want to take it?

The Subconscious Perspective

Are you happy with progression of your goals?
If the answer to this question is no:

Reevaluate your goals. Do you need to upgrade them? If you do upgrade them, make sure you respond to the other statements and question on the Subconscious Perspective in regard to your goals.

Empowering Questions

Have all of your Empowering Questions from the Subconscious Perspective been answered?

If they have not, keep asking and then make sure you write them down. If you have answered all of your questions, are you completely satisfied with the answers? If you are not satisfied with the answers restructure the questions until you are completely satisfied with the answer. For Example: If one of your questions was: "How can I lose this weight?" You my need to enhance it by asking: "What action do I need to take everyday to reach my goal weight and have fun doing it?"

Subconscious Self-Image

Have you been able to maintain your new self-image?
If you have not been able to maintain your new self-image, then this is definitely something you will want to work on in the Stop and Replace System. The issue at the top of the Stop and Replace System would be "Not Maintaining My New Self Image."

The Stop and Replace System

Are you completely happy with the results of the issues you have addressed in the Stop and Replace System?
If the answer to this is no:
Have you been reading this page every day? If the answer to this is no, then you must go back and reread the Stop and Replace System every day for at least a week. If you do not notice a difference, then you need to go back and start a new page with new and better reasons, more powerful questions, and a more compelling replacement picture. Continue the assault on the issue you wish to change until you get what you want and have fully reprogrammed yourself.

Has anything else come up that you need to unlearn?

The Heart of MIND/FITNESS

Have you picked out a minimum of one question per category and are you reading those questions out loud to yourself everyday? This is a minimum you need to do everyday for the rest of your life. Keep in mind that the mind is an incredible multitasking machine so you can ask as many questions as you wish, and it will work on them all.

Food and Fitness Plan

Have there been any foods that were emotionally driven?
If the answer to this is yes, did you address the issue in the Stop and Replace System? If you have not, you need to make an assault on it until you have reprogrammed yourself.

Support System

Once you establish the foundation for reprogramming yourself, it is up to you to implement these tools anytime you discover something that does not work. A client once commented a few months after going through the program that her mind was running amuck. I asked her if she attempted to stop and intervene on the process and the answer of course was no. If you do not intend to continue paying for consultation services, then you need to develop a support system. This is one of the many reasons that the Consultant's Guidelines are included in this book. As I stated earlier: If you do not run it, the mind will run itself.

If you belong to any group, you can introduce MIND/FITNESS by simply printing the Subconscious Perspective (the first page of the Full Spectrum Program) and have your group write down one response to the four statements and one question. In other words ask them to write down one goal, one reason for accomplishing that goal etc. This is what I do when I do a lecture. This is also a good way to learn a small portion of the Consultants Guidelines and test it out. Here again the fundamental question is: What is going to work the best for me?

PART THREE

FOOD & FITNESS
RECOMMENDATIONS

12

Food & Fitness

Recommendations

Which Food Plan

After you have attained emotional control, the question is: What food and fitness plan is going to work the best for me? We will start with the food program. There is not any reason to randomly choose something that has the potential of dramatically affecting your physiology and psychology without first evaluating the science and research of what you are going to choose.

Back in the seventies when the low fat craze began to hit, there was not a bit of scientific evidence that proved what was being sold was accurate and of course we now know it was not. Today is much different. There is reasonably good science behind everything we eat and drink. I say reasonably good because you always need to look at the parameters of scientific tests and who conducts them.

This chapter is only going to address the most fundamental issues of food and fitness because these subjects need their own book which I will do about a year after you see this one. I believe it is important to have the same kind of science behind your food and fitness program that you have behind your MIND/FITNESS program. The problem with everything I look at is that no one seems to start at the beginning. As you may have noticed, I like to start at the beginning.

The beginning for any food program is to eliminate the foods or ingredients to foods that cause the most damage to your body and will impede your success with any food program you choose.

Killing the Sugar Habit

This is the single, most habit forming and destructive food you will have to contend with. Atkins is considered the pioneer in the area of eliminating high sugar producing foods for weight loss. I tried Atkins in the late 70s and it was way too radical for me at that time. The major flaw in Atkins was that there was no differentiation between fats. Milk based products like cheese, butter and of course whole milk is not tightly regulated on this diet.

As of late more studies have been done on high protein, low carb diets, and there is a tremendous number of studies and information on the effects of eliminating grain from your diet. The **Glycemic Index** concept was originally developed by a team of scientists lead by Dr. David Jenkins at the University of Toronto in 1981. The Glycemic Index of a food is the measure of the rise in the level of glucose that occurs in your bloodstream, after that food is ingested.

This is important because when you eat foods with a high glycemic index, your blood sugar levels increase to a point of causing a significant physiological change.

The rise in blood sugar causes your pancreas to secrete insulin, which is your body's way of getting your blood sugar level back to normal.

This excessive secretion of insulin will:

- Cause your body to store excess sugar as fat.
- Inhibits the "burning" of previously stored fat, and
- Signals our liver to make cholesterol!
- Causes an eventual insulin resistance that can lead to type II diabetes.

As foods with a low glycemic index (G.I.) are absorbed more slowly, the calories from the food you eat are more likely to be burned throughout the day as energy, rather than stored as fat. Studies have shown that even when calorie intake is the same, you can lose more weight eating low G.I. foods rather than high G.I. foods. Jenkins found that foods such as potatoes traditionally defined as a complex carbohydrate actually led to a rapid rise in blood sugar. Some foods high in simple carbohydrates appeared to digest more slowly, leading to a gradual elevation in blood sugar.

The Glycemic Index of a food is derived by comparing the rate of digestion to that food, with the rate of digestion of pure glucose. Glucose is assigned a Glycemic Index of 100, and the tested food is charted against this standard. Glucose is the most widely accepted reference food; however some other systems use white bread instead.

Foods with a high Glycemic Index (70 and above) are those that break down quickly and cause a spike in blood sugar levels. Foods with a low Glycemic Index (55 and below) break down more slowly and steadily, resulting in a more sustained supply of energy.

Having a basic understanding of this index is important in more ways than one.

If you have a sugar habit now in the form of high sugar content foods such as cakes, candies, ice cream or chocolate, it is going to be difficult to kill if you are also eating foods high on the glycemic index.

Women's bodies scream for chocolate when premenstrual food cravings surface. Researchers argue that this craving is because chocolate contains high levels of magnesium and prior to menstruation women's bodies experience magnesium deficiency. The problem is that for chocolate to be palatable it has to be loaded with sugar. My suggestion is to find another source of magnesium. Most good calcium contains magnesium, and I will be talking about vitamins later in this chapter.

There is a relatively new way to assess the impact of carbohydrate consumption called the glycemic load that takes the glycemic index into account. This gives a fuller picture than does glycemic index alone. I am not going to include that here for reasons of keeping things simple, but you do need to be aware of it in case you wish to take things a bit further. A GI value tells you only how rapidly a particular carbohydrate turns into sugar. It does not tell you how much of that carbohydrate is in a serving of a particular food. The carbohydrate in watermelon, for example, has a high GI. But there is not a lot of it, so watermelon's glycemic load is relatively low. A GL of 20 or more is high, a GL of 11 to 19 inclusive is medium, and a GL of 10 or less is low.

There are a couple of flaws with the glycemic index, and I will explain them in a moment. The bottom line here is that you need to have an idea or baseline about how your body processes certain types of foods.

The problem with the glycemic index is that you do not know how empty or full or the type of food the person had in their system when the blood sugar per each food was measured. The other problem is that the sugar content in some fruits increases as it gets ripe.

There are also more up to date glycemic indexes. This one just happens to be the one the majority of people are using who are writing low carb books. It is important that you kill your sugar habit before going on a high protein diet.

I do not endorse limitations of fruits or vegetables with any diet except those that are exceptionally high on the glycemic index. These types of carbohydrates are essential if you want what you have eaten to pass all the way through your system. You must find a balance from the beginning. Grains on the other hand are different. We have only been eating grains for the past ten thousand years, and our bodies simply have not adjusted to them so a significant reduction in the amount of grains you eat will only benefit you.

Following is the glycemic index. It will give you a basic idea of how foods are rated in regard to their sugar output once you eat them.

The Glycemic Index

Beans

Food	Glycemic Index
Baby lima	32
Black Bean	30
Butter Bean	31
Kidney Bean	27
Pinto Bean	42
Split Peas	32
Baked Bean	43
Brown Bean	38
Chickpeas	33
Navy Bean	38
Red Lentils	27
Soy Beans	18

Breads

Food	Glycemic Index
Bagel	72
Pita	57
Rye	64
White	72
Waffles	76

The Glycemic Index

Breads

Food	Glycemic Index
Kaiser roll	73
Pumpernickel	49
Rye, whole	50
Whole wheat	72

Desserts

Food	Glycemic Index
Angel food cake	67
Danish	59
Pound Cake	54
Bran muffin	60
Fruit bread	47
Sponge Cake	46

Fruit

Food	Glycemic Index
Apple	38
Apricot, dried	30
Banana, unripe	30
Fruit cocktail	55

The Glycemic Index

Fruit

Food	Glycemic Index
Grapes	43
Mango	55
Pear	36
Plum	24
Strawberries	32
Apricot, canned	64
Banana	62
Cherries	22
Grapefruit	25
Kiwi	52
Orange	43
Pineapple	66
Raisins	64
Watermelon	72

Grains

Food	Glycemic Index
Barley	22
Buckwheat	54
Chickpeas	36

The Glycemic Index

Grains

Food	Glycemic Index
Hominy	40
Rice, instant	91
Rye	34
Wheat, whole	41
Amylose	59
Brown rice	59
Bulgur	47
Cornmeal	68
Millet	75
Rice, parboiled	47
Sweet corn	55
Rice, white	HIGH

Juices

Food	Glycemic Index
Apple	41
Orange	55
Grapefruit	48
Pineapple	46

The Glycemic Index

Milk Products

Food	Glycemic Index
Chocolate milk	34
Milk	34
Ice cream	50
Yogurt	38

Pasta

Food	Glycemic Index
Brown rice pasta	92
Macaroni	46
Spaghetti	40
Vermicelli	35
Linguine, Durham	50
Macaroni & cheese	64
Spaghetti, protein enriched	28

Just a reminder that everything in this chapter is a recommendation, I am just presenting to you the current science on food and fitness. The primary question will always be: Which food and Fitness Plan is going to work the best for me?

There have been many low carb books over the past few years like *Sugar Busters*, *The Zone*, *The Protein Power Life Plan*, *The South Beach Diet* and of course *The Atkins New Diet Revolution*. The popularity of these books went way up when legitimate studies were done on the Atkins diet that proved what he had been preaching for the last 30 years was indeed true.

In research financed by the Robert C. Atkins foundation in New York City, which promotes the Atkins diet, Dr. Eric Westman of Duke University studied 120 overweight volunteers. They were randomly assigned to the Atkins diet or the American Heart Association's Step 1 diet, a widely used low-fat approach. On the Atkins diet, people limited their carb's to less than 20 grams a day, and 60 percent of their calories came from fat.

After six months, the people on the Atkins diet had lost 31 pounds, compared with 20 pounds on the AHA (American Heart Association) diet, and more people stuck with the Atkins regimen. Total cholesterol fell slightly in both groups. However, those on the Atkins diet had an 11 percent increase in HDL, the good cholesterol, and a 49 percent drop in triglycerides. On the AHA diet, HDL was unchanged, and triglycerides dropped 22 percent. High (LDL) triglycerides may raise the risk of heart disease. While the volunteers' total amounts of LDL, the bad cholesterol, did not change much on either diet, there was evidence that it had shifted to a form that may be less likely to clog the arteries.

As I said in an earlier chapter, all diets have the same fail rate including the low carb diets. The message here is to go in with the right mind set and maintain that mind set until you are confident you have reprogrammed yourself. If you have not taken control of your subconscious programming before you start, your chances of success at anything will be significantly diminished.

The best books on the current list of low carb diets are *The Protein Power Life Plan* by Michael and Mary Eades and *The South Beach Diet* by Arthur Agatston, MD. These are two very different books in there approach. My favorite is *The Protein Power Life Plan* because it is detailed and very comprehensive. It is 434 pages not including a 26 page introduction. You can shorten that up a bit by skipping the chapter on exercise. It is a relatively heavy read but well worth it. *The South Beach Diet* is a much lighter read at 320 pages with half the book dedicated to recipes. Neither book addresses eating as a behavior.

Ingredients to Eliminate Right Now

There are several ingredients to foods that you need to watch for right now. Starting a different way of eating is one of the hardest things you will ever do and you will need to pace yourself so that the implementation is permanent. One of the most basic things you can do as a permanent first step is to eliminate a couple of the nastiest ingredients that are listed below.

High Fructose Corn Sweetener - High-fructose corn syrup (HFCS) is more easily turned into fat than any other carbohydrate. And it's everywhere, from the obvious places like sodas to barbecue sauce and canned soup. HFCS is different from other sugars and sweeteners, which can make you fat indirectly over time. HFCS makes you fat by the straightest possible metabolic path. Some are making a correlation with this sweetener that was introduced in the 70s and the rise in obesity in the 80s and 90s.

The problem with HFCS is the fructose, a sugar that occurs naturally in fruit and honey rather than the corn syrup. High-fructose corn syrup is a cheap and doubly sweet chemical derivative.

Your body doesn't necessarily use fructose as an immediate source of energy. "Fructose is more readily metabolized into fat," says Peter Havel, PhD, a nutrition researcher at the University of California at Davis. Havel is among a growing number of scientists who suspect that there's a connection between fructose and America's skyrocketing rates of obesity and diabetes. I am not saying the small amounts of fructose you get through fruit or honey will make you fat. Fruit is packed with vitamins, minerals, and fiber, all of which are components of a healthy diet.

HFCS is about 20% cheaper than cane sugar which has made it easier for manufacturers to super size their portions. Read nutrition labels. Start with the ingredients and do not buy the food if it contains this chemically produced ingredient.

Aspartame - Russell L. Blaylock, MD has written the most comprehensive book on this additive called *Excitotoxins: The Taste That Kills*. In it he explains how brain damage can be caused by this additive.

Aspartame is a molecule made by joining two amino acids together; in other words, it is a tiny protein fragment. It can enter the bloodstream intact and find its way though the circulation to a vulnerable area of the brain called the bare area, where it can gain entry to the brain. Its chemical structure allows it to fit into a receptor within the brain called the NMDA (N-methyl-d-aspartate) receptor, triggering such over stimulation in the nerve cell that it dies. In other words, the brain cell literally becomes excited to death.

Reports in medical literature suggest that in susceptible people, consuming aspartame may result in symptoms such as mood disturbances, sleep disturbances, headaches, dizziness, short-term memory loss, fuzzy thinking and inability to concentrate. Some in the scientific community suspect that the excitotoxic effect may lead to permanent damage of the brain and nervous system.

Hydrogenated Oils - Also known as trans-fatty acids, this form of oil has been appropriately nick named artery glue. A diet high in trans-fats appears to be unhealthier than a diet that is just high in saturated fats. A diet high in trans-fats can reduce normal blood vessel function by nearly one-third and reduce HDL cholesterol, the so-called good cholesterol by more than 20%. All of this of course leads to a predisposition to heart attack and stroke.

I know this list could be a lot more comprehensive but I am only going to address the most fundamental issues here or what I consider to be the absolute minimum you must do in regard to your food and fitness plan. In diet speak this is Step 1. When you can consistently maintain this one simple step, then you are ready for Step 2. There is no need to go wild if you cannot do this first simple step.

The Fitness Plan

There are a tremendous number of variables when choosing a fitness plan. I will address the most important ones first. You always see a disclaimer at the beginning of every fitness book and on every fitness product, and this is for good reason. If you have never been in a structured fitness program, you have to be told so here it goes. Be sure to check with your physician before starting or significantly increasing your exercise schedule so that you fully understand what your body can tolerate.

When Dr. Brenner and I started Lifestyle Systems in the mid eighties, we had all the bases covered, and I will go over some of them here.

Blood Pressure - If you do not know what your blood pressure is, you must find out. Ultimately you need to know what it is at an elevated heart rate. If you are overweight and on blood pressure medication, I do not recommend lifting weights until you have reduced your weight to under 10% of what is considered the maximum for your gender and/or regained control of your blood pressure without medication. Proper breathing is important for everyone but especially for you. Anytime you hold your breath, your blood pressure goes up.

Fitness trainers may not be as aware of this subject as they should be; so it is up to you to manage it should you decide to get into a lifting program. A baseline fitness program is recommended which I will lay out after addressing these basic physiological issues.

Resting Heart Rate - This one is easy to check on your own by just learning to take your pulse at rest. This is one of the many numbers that will improve with a consistent aerobic program.

Oxygen Uptake - This is an issue that must be taken up with your pulmonologist if you suffer from asthma or exercise induced asthma. You need to consult with your pulmonologist if you intend to start an aerobic program and you have either of these problems.

Range of Motion - This is something that you may not realize is a problem until you have pulled a muscle. Depending on your age, gender, and the type of work you do, your body may not be symmetrical. The best way to find out is to have a fitness trainer (if they are trained in the use of a goniometer) or a physical therapist do a range of motion test. You can test yourself to an extent by just paying more attention during your stretch or yoga class. Stretching of course needs to be an integral part of your overall fitness regime.

Gait - Gait refers to how you walk. This is important to assess if you plan on getting into a walking program or especially a running program. When you walk, you naturally supinate and pronate. This means that your foot strikes the outer edge of your shoe heel and then the path of the foot follows a diagonal line across the bottom of the foot and you push off at the area of your first and second toe. If you have some flat shoes that you have broken in, you can see if your gait is normal or not. In the eighties the number one injury for runners was over-pronation. The primary reason for this was that it was difficult to find a running shoe that followed the natural path of the gait. Most running shoes had an indentation in the center of the heel. When the foot would strike the outer edge of the heel, it would quickly try to adjust to the shoe and over-pronation would occur.

Blood Panel - If you are changing your food and fitness program, this is highly recommended. There are a variety of blood panels that you can do and that you may need to do depending on your age and gender. It is important to establish a baseline so that you can monitor your improvement. The minimum you need to do is a cardiovascular profile which includes the following.

CARDIOVASCULAR RISK PROFILE	
Total Cholesterol	Cholesterol/HDL Ratio
HDL Cholesterol	Estimated CHD Risk
LDL Cholesterol	Glucose
Triglycerides	Iron

Minimum Fitness Recommendations

Aerobic - The minimum that you need to do to establish aerobic fitness is a minimum of 20 minutes three times a week at your working heart rate. Your working heart rate is calculated by starting with 220 subtract your age and then sixty to seventy percent of that.

Remember that aerobic means with oxygen so this can mean many different things. If you have a problem with your gait, then a bike or stair master might be appropriate. If you do not have any problems with your gait, then there are many options. Your choice of shoes will be an important decision. If you are wheel chair bound, then you need to find a gym with an arm ergometer. This is a bicycle that you pedal with your arms.

Shoes - The very first thing to look for in a shoe is: Does it follow the natural path of the gait? This is especially important if you intend to run in them. The second is: Can you remove the insole? This is a huge comfort issue because the insole of most running shoes is flattened within a couple of weeks. I use the Spenco cross trainer insole because it is the most comfortable for me and it will last through more than one pair of shoes. There are others so do your homework. Injury prevention is going to be one of your biggest concerns so make sure you do it right and shop around.

Crunches - These used to be called sit-ups. The old sit up however required that you sit all the way up from a lying down position. Doing this enacted the psoas muscle which affected the lower back. The term crunch came about to describe a more concentrated sit up that simply stopped at the end of the range of the upper abs, and thus you did not sit up all the way.

The importance of an abdominal workout that affects all the muscles in your mid section can not be over emphasized. Back injuries and pain from working out are in large part a result of weak abs. All movement needs to be thought of as originating from your center (your abs). Establishing strength in this area is the absolute first thing you must do.

Lifting

Lifting weights can be down right dangerous if you do not do some evaluation on yourself before you start. The very first thing of course, as I stated previously, is to know what your blood pressure is and consult with your physician even if it is borderline. Never hold your breadth while you lift, high blood pressure or not.

The next biggest issue is form. Until your form is absolutely perfect, I do not recommend using anything heavier than 2 to 5 pounds if any weight at all. For this reason alone, you will want to use a certified fitness trainer to initiate a lifting program. It does not make any sense to enthusiastically start out lifting and then injure yourself before you have a chance to begin the process of reshaping your body.

It is imperative that you start out slowly and increase your weights slowly and consistently. In the mid 80s when I was working with Dr. Brenner, our formula was 70% of one maximum rep. In other words if you could do one maximum rep of 70 lbs on the bench press, 70% of that would equal 12 to 16 reps. I recommend doing a pyramid that starts with 16 reps. From there you add 2.5 to 10lbs depending on what you are doing and lower the reps by two with each set. Your first set would be 16 reps, second set would be 14 reps, and your third set would be 12. I know 16 reps seem high initially but the bottom line when starting is injury prevention. Again I know this is a very light overview of lifting, but you need some place to start.

Sleep

Sleep is a very fundamental issue when taking control of your emotional state and your food and fitness plan. You are in a weakened state when you have not had enough sleep. There are also significant physiological issues that will cause you to drift from your objectives, and this is why it is crucial that you recognize when you have not had enough sleep and use MIND/FITNESS to stay focused and to get through those tough days when you are sleep deprived the night before. There will be times when you will need to chant this question: "How can I keep myself up, on, centered, and focused." *and* "What do I need to do to stay focused?"

Leptin is a molecule secreted by fat cells and conveys a satiety signal. "There's enough fuel on board." With sleep restriction the body says, "I need more food." which may lead to overeating. When you're sleep-deprived, you want to go for an empty calorie energy boost and usually those are carbohydrates that are very low in nutrients and very high in calories. The body sees sleep deprivation as a state of stress; cortisol is the stress hormone. Cortisol causes, in turn, the release of insulin.

The key question here is: "How can I make sure I get a good night sleep?" There are many variables to this question, but one that most people do not consider is caffeine. DrBobMartin.com has a good article on caffeine. In it he states that caffeine has a half life of 4 hours and twenty five percent of the caffeine is still in the body after twelve hours. This in of itself could keep you from getting a deep sleep. Even if you do not remember waking up during the night, you may not be getting a good rem sleep. There are no studies in regard to caffeine and rem sleep, but clients that have taken the advice to cut back on their caffeine intake or eliminate it all together have had positive results. There are many problems with caffeine; one of which is that it stimulates the pancreas to produce insulin. The issue with understanding the glycemic index is to keep your insulin production under control, and there are many more variables other than food that you need to take into consideration. I have had prescribed pharmaceuticals that effect my nervous system less than one cup of Starbuck's coffee. The list of negative affects of coffee and caffeine is long, but I want to focus on the most important one here…and that is the effect it may have on your sleep. Green tea is a good alternative; it does have caffeine in it, just not the extraordinary amounts that your local specialty coffee shops may have. It is estimated that it has the same amount as a cup of decaf coffee. You can get decaf green tea and the benefits of green tea are as long as the negatives for coffee, one of which is a dramatic improvement in the immune system.

Supplements

Part of the program developed with Dr. Brenner in the mid 80s was the use of a software program that broke down over ten thousand foods into 58 vitamins and minerals. I worked with this program for over a month to create a diet that would eliminate the use of vitamins. The conclusion was that unless you liked eating a lot of raw oysters every day, it is impossible to get all the vitamins and minerals you need for optimum health. The question is then not whether you should take supplements but which ones.

It is imperative that you evaluate the science behind any decision you make that could have a dramatic affect on your physiology or psychology. With this in mind I can only recommend one supplement and that is Shaklee Vita-Lea. Even though I do not like the way this supplement is marketed, it has the most scientific data behind it.

It is the only multivitamin that I am aware of that has data on how much of the vitamin is actually absorbed into the body. This of course is the most fundamental issue when taking a supplement. You could be paying more for a discount vitamin if it is not absorbed. Vita-Lea also includes pricier ingredients like folic acid and biotin which many other multivitamins do not. I have been using Vita-Lea since the mid seventies, but I have never sold it. I simply want the best supplement so I endure a marketing structure I do not particularly care for to get what I feel is the best. One thing to look for when buying supplements is whether it comes with iron or not.

A Word about Your Weight

I frequently see ads that say: Lose 14 pounds in 14 days or lose 30 pounds in thirty days. The American College of sports medicine has set standards internationally for weight loss through years of clinical studies. They indicate that you can not safely lose more than a kilogram per week which is 2.2 pounds, without risking the loss of calorie burning muscle mass.

After you understand how to control your eating behavior, simply ask yourself: What food and fitness plan will work the best for me? A much more extensive breakdown of what your food and fitness plan should look like will be available in an upcoming book. It will also be broken down into steps so that you can advance at a pace that is comfortable for you. The information in this chapter is the most fundamental for your first step to a more refined food and fitness plan.

APPENDICES

Appendix A

Consultants Guidelines

How to Use the Guidelines

The Consultants Guidelines are laid out in **7 Steps** and 8 sections, with the last section dedicated to Follow Up. If you print out the Guidelines from the CD, there is a break between each step and you will put a tab from your 8 tab set just before this break. The notebook is laid out in 5 sections and will be identified as **Section 1**, **Section 2** and so on.

You will notice two headings, **"Note"** and **"CONSULTANT"**. Anytime you see **"Note"** I am speaking to you. Anytime you see **"CONSULTANT,"** this is you speaking to the client. There will always be people who are more comfortable taking the lead and people who are more comfortable participating. If you have decided to take the lead, then you need to learn these guidelines just as you would a script. A good way to learn this script is to thoroughly put yourself through the program once a week for a month. If you are going to take a leading role, you need to be able to use the Guidelines only as a reference while maintaining as much eye contact with the person or persons you are working with.

Through the course of the program process, you will ask if anyone would like to volunteer some of the information they have written down; however, you do not have to have information from the client in order for the program to work. The client needs to know that the notebook is for their eyes only unless they wish to share the information. If you are working with a minor, the parents need to be informed of this and need to respect the wishes of the child in regard to the information they write down in the notebook.

The reason for publishing these Guidelines and allowing access to them after 14 years is simple. There are so many people who are absolutely lost if they have a friend, child or someone they care about who is out of control. Providing these Guidelines along with the **Program** will give anyone who needs it the opportunity to take control of their lives.

Note:

Before you start, always make sure the person or people you are working with fill out the Emotional Checklist. The Guidelines are set up to do the Program in one or two sessions and to focus on the full spectrum (Love, Health, Wealth, and Self-Image). If you plan on doing a single session, it will take approximately 3 to 4 hours. Two sessions will take approximately 2 hours each. The amount of time varies, depending on age, gender and how well the consultant knows the program. The Guidelines indicate where you can split the Program. Follow up on the program can and needs to be done for a minimum of 30 days. MIND/FITNESS techniques must be used everyday.

First, introduce yourself and thank the individual or group for being there. If you have a large group, use name tags so you can refer to each client by name. Always start out by explaining the Program, how it works, and how the client will benefit.

Ultimately it is better if your clients fill out the emotional checklist before attending a workshop. The Emotional Checklist needs to be saved from the CD that accompanies the book to the client's hard drive. From there they fill it out and then send it as an attachment to your email address. Always keep plenty of copies of the checklist just in case. For the most comprehensive monitoring of the client, you will want them to fill out another one 24 hours after the workshop and then once per week after that for 30 days.

Step 1 - The Emotional Checklist

CONSULTANT

The program process of MIND/FITNESS is done in 7 steps. The first step is to establish a baseline which will allow you and I to understand where you are emotionally right now, your understanding of how a behavior works, and how satisfied you are with your relationships. All of this will improve dramatically with the use of MIND/FITNESS. Is there anyone who has not filled out the Emotional Checklist?

Note:

If there is anyone who has not filled out the Emotional Checklist, give them a copy to fill out while you explain the program.

CONSULTANT

If you have a goal or an objective in your life, is the beginning usually a good place to start? The obvious answer is yes. Yet, when it comes to issues with the body or any other issue, you are being convinced by companies who make billions of dollars each year on medication and other products that you can skip the processes of the mind and simply attack the body. This is going to stop right here right now! You are convinced that it is always about the answer without fully considering what the question needs to be in order to produce the results you want. If you do not start out with the right question, you may not get the answer that is going to work the best for you. You will learn with the program process of MIND/FITNESS that your questions are at the very core of getting what you want or what you do not want!

With this in mind, we will start with the most fundamental question for initiating any change you wish to make permanent in your life. What determines your emotional state and behavior? What determines your emotional state and behavior is just **information**. The next question then would be: What are the components of this information? The two components of the information that determines your emotional state and behavior are words and pictures. The next question then is: "How do I access and change this information so that I can permanently change the way I feel and take control of my behavior?"

Are you with me so far? All you have to understand is how to **Recognize**, **Access** and

Change the information that determines your emotional state and behavior in order to produce different results. This is what MIND/ FITNESS is going to do for you. This of course brings up the next question. What is MIND/FITNESS? MIND/FITNESS is the clinically proven process of changing your subconscious programming to match your conscious goals. Why is it important to change your subconscious programming to match your conscious goals?

Think back to your last New Year's resolution. Consciously you wanted to make a change, but you probably did not take into consideration the solidly planted subconscious programming that determines the behavior you want to change.

To give you an idea of the power of the subconscious, you can speak at a rate of about two to three hundred words per minute. Your subconscious runs at a rate of about one thousand to twelve hundred words per minute which is about four times faster than what you can speak. This is why you can talk on the phone and perform other tasks like typing on the computer or driving a car because the subconscious is already programmed to do the other tasks.

You can look at the conscious mind and the subconscious mind like a tug of war with a vat of mud in the middle for whomever loses.

The conscious mind is one-person on one side against the subconscious, which are four people on the other side.

If the conscious decides to move in a different direction like losing weight, increasing your exercise program, quitting smoking or any number of other things, it is usually a losing proposition because you are simply out numbered with information. This is why it is so difficult to attain spontaneous change. Evidence of this is with the approximately 98% fail rate for people who do not maintain a desired weight loss.

Is it important that you know what is going on in the subconscious? Yes, it is imperative if you want to change something in your life and you want it to be permanent. MIND/ FITNESS is based on the reality that all behavior is emotionally driven or in other words, your emotional state = your behavior. How you feel about things you do will always determine whether you move toward your goals or not. You will always move toward pleasure and away from pain. So the key component of any behavior change program should always include how to get control of your emotional state. The program process of MIND/FITNESS is going to make sure you have the most people on your side in the tug of war.

What is the biggest difference between

MIND/FITNESS and any other behavior change program? The question MIND/FITNESS asks is: "How can I fix it?" As opposed to: "Why is it broken?" Burris MIND/FITNESS does not tell you what to do; it guides you through the process of how to get it done.

Note:

This is a good time to give a sample of an emotionally driven behavior. One of my personal favorites is a time when I was explaining my program to a gentleman who responded: "I am doing a technique that is based on pure logic. I am training myself to respond to every situation in a purely logical manner with no emotion involved. I find that it has worked better for me than anything else I have ever tried."

As he was explaining this to me, his voice was monotone and his face was almost expressionless. When he completed his explanation, I asked him how he felt about this method and his eyes got real big He smiled, and said "GREAT."

CONSULTANT

If you do not know how to create change in your emotional state, its like riding in the back seat of a car with some maniac going all over the road. MIND/FITNESS will guide you through the process of how to get rid of the maniac that is currently driving and get you behind the wheel of your emotional state and your behavior. When you identify something that does not work for you such as fear, guilt, anger, hopelessness, etc., you simply unlearn it and replace it with something that works better. How are you going to do this, you might ask? On the first page of the program, you will put your subconscious on paper. You will then use that information to begin an assault on what simply does not work which in turn will change your emotional state and behaviors that do not work for you. The reason you must write everything down is because if you do not, how are you going to know where you have started, where you are going, or where you have ended? It is also the only way you can track your progress.

The way you feel about things in your life is determined by your individual perception, so I would like to start out by making a change in your perception. Have you ever failed at anything? Within the context of MIND/FITNESS, there is no such thing as failure, there are only **results**. If you do not like the results you are getting, you simply change what you are doing. With MIND/FITNESS you continue to bend, shape, rearrange, and change the programming in the subconscious until you achieve the external results you want.

Until now you have been programmed to attack the body to try to change your mind. You were made to believe that someone else will take control of your behavior by simply telling you what to do while you passively sit back. This is part of your programming you need to overcome in order to take control of your subconscious programming. Permanent positive change can only occur if you understand, are willing to find out how the mind works, and then use that information to take control.

Note:

If your client or clients are using the notebook to write in, the first page should have the three-hole punch on the opposite side so that the first two pages of the notebook face each other. If you are doing a teleworkshop or a workshop where everyone is using a computer, you can use the bookmark tab to negotiate through the sections and the page tab to negotiate through the pages. The guidelines are written with the assumption that you are using a printed notebook. Simply change your direction if using the online version.

CONSULTANT

Let's take a quick look at the notebook contents. The notebook is divided into 5 sections. Please open your notebook to section 1.

Section 1 - Subconscious Perspective

The first section contains three pages. This is where you literally put the subconscious on paper and lay out the foundation for the rest of the program. The first two pages are **Step 2** of the program process which addresses how you speak to yourself on the deepest level of the subconscious. Page three addresses your subconscious pictures and the structure of how you store them.

Section 2 - Stop and Replace Samples

Let's go to section 2. These are samples of the stop and replace system, which you can use during an assault on a particular habit, behavior or emotional state that you **Absolutely Must** change.

Section 3 - The Stop and Replace System

Let's go to section 3, The Stop and Replace System. This is the fourth step and the most powerful part of the program. These are the blank Stop and Replace sheets that will allow you to make an assault on any programming that does not work for you by using the same process that created the program.

All the elements from the first three pages of the program are used on this page to help you **Recognize**, **Access** and **Change** subconscious programming that does not work for you.

Section 4 - The Heart of MIND/FITNESS

Let's take a look at section 4, The Heart of MIND/FITNESS. You will use this part of the program to maintain your minimum MIND/ FITENSS after you have completed the program. As it states on the first page, it is imperative that you ask yourself at least one question per category when you get up in the morning and when you go to bed at night. You will also ask yourself the five key questions as you go through your day. **On to section 5.**

Section 5 - Food and Fitness Planner

This is your Food and Fitness Planner. Why include this in a program for the mind? This is included because what you eat, drink and your level of fitness have a lot to do in determining how you feel. In other words, you do not want to risk your body taking over your mind. I will get more into the details of each section as we go through the program.

The information you write down in your notebook is for your eyes only unless you choose to share something. Let's flip back to section one and get started.

Step 2 - Subconscious Perspective and Empowering Questions

Section 1

The components of the information that drive you are words and pictures. The first two pages of the Program is Step 2 which addresses the first component...your words. Let's get started with the Subconscious Perspective.

Subconscious Perspective - Page 1

1) Please write down all the goals you **ABSOLUTELY MUST** accomplish.

I will be asking you questions about the categories that we will be working on to generate as much information as possible.

Accomplishing your goals is all about your mind set. The initial mind set before you write down your goals need to be clearly defined. You clearly define your initial mind set in relation to your goals with two key words, and they are **ABSOLUTE MUST**. Before you write down a goal, it must be clearly defined in your mind as an **ABSOLUTE MUST.** For example: You absolutely must eat and drink to stay alive and similar absolute musts in your life.

Questions for your Love
A) Do I need to be more respectful and loving toward my family?
B) Do I need to improve my listening habits and time together?

C) Do I need to become more spiritually centered and establish a greater sense of purpose and inner peace?

Questions for your Health

A) Do I need to lose weight, upgrade my appearance, increase my work out program, improve nutrition or increase the regularity of medical check ups?

B) Do I need to have a greater level of control over my emotional state and behavior?

Questions for your Wealth

A) Do I need to increase my job satisfaction, purpose and confidence?

B) Do I need to fulfill the divine design of my life?

C) Do I need to increase earnings, savings and budget my money better?

Questions for your Self-Image

A) Do I need to improve my sense of humor?

B) Do I need to improve my ability to communicate?

C) Do I need to improve my self-confidence?

D) Do I need to improve my self-esteem and self-worth?

Full Spectrum goal questions

A) What other goals can I think of that I ABSOLUTELY MUST accomplish?

B) What goals can I think of that would give me tremendous pleasure if accomplished?

C) What other goals would I like to acquire but feel may be too difficult?

Note:

Pay close attention to the response of this next statement because it will indicate whether a client is ready to change.

CONSULTANT

Are you ready to move on to statement 2?

2) Please write down the reasons why you feel you **ABSOLUTELY MUST** accomplish your goals.

Questions for Statement 2

A) How will the accomplishment of my goals affect my income?

B) How will accomplishing my goals affect my personal and professional relationships?

C) Will I feel more spiritually centered?

D) Will I feel a greater sense of power and control over my emotional state and behavior?

E) Are there medical or health reasons for accomplishing my goals?

F) How will the accomplishment of these goals affect my self-confidence?

Are you ready to move on to statement 3?

3) Please write down what you feel you **ABSOLUTELY MUST** do to accomplish your goals.

Questions for Statement 3
A) Do I feel I need to manage my time better?
B) Do I feel I need to spend more time in meditation or prayer?
C) Do I feel I need to be more honest with my family, friends or co-workers?
D) Do I feel I need a personal trainer?

Are you ready to move on to statement 4?

Right now excuses are the barriers that are keeping you from what you want. It is important however to think of as many excuses as you possibly can because you are going to find out how to use these excuses to help you move you toward your new goals.

4) Please write down all of the excuses that keep you from attaining your goals.

Questions for Statement 4
A) Do you use a friend or family member as an excuse?
B) Do I use my work situation or time as one of my excuses?

C) Do I use any medical problems as an excuse?

D) Do I use the weather or cost and distance from the health club as an excuse?

E) Do I feel a lack of will power has kept me from accomplishing my goals?

F) Do I use my past failures as an excuse?

Are you ready to move on to question 5?

Before you respond to this question I need to ask you a question. Do you ask yourself questions? Yes.

You ask yourself questions on an ongoing basis and those questions to yourself begin as soon as you get up each morning. You ask questions like: What do I need to do today? What am I going to wear? Whom do I need to call? Where are my keys? With this in mind...

5) Do you feel confident you can accomplish your goals, and if not, what questions do you ask about them? (Please write down at least one question per goal)

A question for question 5

A) If you do not currently ask yourself questions about your goals, what questions would you ask yourself if you did?

When you are done, please go back to the top of the page and I will explain to you what you have just done.

Statement 1

1) Please write down all the goals you **ABSOLUTELY MUST** accomplish.

Why do you set goals? You set goals to give the mind some place to go; otherwise, it will choose something on its own.

Do you ever get in your car and start driving without a destination? Maybe sometimes you do, but even then at some point, you have to establish a destination or goal even if it is to just stop and get more gas.

The two key words when establishing your goals is of course, **ABSOLUTELY MUST**. **On to statement 2**

Statement 2

2) Please write down the reasons why you feel you **ABSOLUTELY MUST** accomplish your goals.

We refer to your reasons for accomplishing your goals as **Anchors** which are what attach you to any one particular behavior. So first you give the mind somewhere to go and then you anchor yourself to those new goals to assure that you will keep moving toward them. Excuses are also anchors, but they are keeping you attached to what you do not want.

In just a minute I'm going to show you how to use those excuses as a fast moving vehicle that will move you toward your goal instead of keeping you away from your goals, which is what they are doing now. I want you to take a quick look at your goals, and if you are unable to think of a good reason for accomplishing that goal, draw a line through it until you are able to think of a good reason for accomplishing that goal.

On to statement 3

Statement 3

3) Please write down what you feel you **ABSOLUTELY MUST** do to accomplish your goals.

Writing down what you need to do to accomplish your goals is like making a map. You always need to clearly define what action needs to be taken in order to get from point A to point B.

It is also important because you can turn that map into empowering questions, which will accelerate the process of your goals. I will explain empowering questions with statement four.

Statement 4

4) Please write down all of the excuses that keep you from attaining your goals.

Before we get started on excuses, I need to ask you a question: Does your subconscious mind work on questions when you're not consciously involved? Yes!

Have ever asked yourself the question: What is that person's name? You may not get an answer right away, but maybe in an hour or two or even the next day while you are doing something totally unrelated, the answer comes popping into your head as clear as day. The mind will work on and produce a response to absolutely every question you ask yourself.

What does this have to do with excuses? **If you turn your excuse into a positive empowering question and continue to repeat it as a question, the mind will no longer be able to use it as an excuse.** For example: If one of your excuses is time, you can turn that excuse into a question such as: How can I find more time to spend on my food and fitness program and have a good time with it?

If you continue to repeat this as a question, the mind will no longer be able to use it as an excuse. What you have done is not only pull that anchor up, but it has also become a high-speed vehicle to move you more quickly toward your goals. **On to Question 5**

Question 5

5) Do you feel confident you can accomplish your goals, and if not, what questions do you ask about them?

Why is this question a key component in regard to your subconscious? When I ask you a question, what part of your consciousness usually gives you a response? You have to retrieve an answer from the subconscious. If I ask you a question about questions that you ask yourself, you have now gained access to the deepest level of the subconscious, as we know it. This is the very beginning of the process that brings about an emotional state, which in turn determines your behavior. This is why it is important to ask yourself at least one question per goal. It helps you to understand how you communicate with yourself in relationship to that goal on the deepest level of the subconscious.

Now that you know the mind works on questions when you are not consciously involved, how important then does the structure of the questions you ask yourself become? It becomes very important, because if you are now asking yourself questions like: "Why can't I maintain a consistent exercise program?" *or* "Why can't I stop eating unhealthy foods?" *or* "Why can't I accomplish my goals?" What do you think the results of these questions will be? They will give you more excuses or keep you anchored to what you do not want.

If you have any questions down that have a don't or can't in them, these questions will be turned into **Empowering Questions** such as: "How can I keep myself on a consistent fitness program and have a good time doing it?" *or* "How can I make sure that I eat only foods that work for me?" *or* "What action do I need to take to make sure I am always moving quickly toward my goals?"

If you are not happy with the results you are getting, changing the questions you ask yourself is the first thing you absolutely must do consistently if you what to make a change. There are five key questions that you will be asking yourself every day. We will go over these when we get to **Step 5.**

Do you have any Questions? On to Page 2, **Empowering Questions**

Note:

When someone tells you that something does not work for them, you simply ask them: What will work for you? The client or patient will then tell you the changes they need to make and you simply comply.

This is one of the many reasons that this is the most powerful program for behavior change. How many people have you ever worked with who will encourage you to scrutinize them or their services so closely?

CONSULTANT

Empowering Questions - Page 2

Please turn all of your responses from page 1 of the **Subconscious Perspective** into positive empowering questions on this page.

Note:

Begin from the goal category at the top of the Subconscious Perspective. Ask someone to volunteer a goal that you can help them with. Most **Empowering Questions** will begin with: "How can I" *or* "What actions do I need to take to" *or* "What do I need to do to? " For example: If one of your client's goals was to lose 25 pounds and maintain a more consistent fitness program, an empowering question to this might be: How can I **permanently** lose 25 pounds and have more fun with my fitness program?

Why questions are usually put in a negative context but you can also use why questions if phrased properly. For example: You can change: "Why am I so fat?" *or* "Why can't I stop eating unhealthy foods?" *or* "Why can't I seem to maintain my motivation?" *to* "Why am I in such incredibly good shape?" *or* "Why am I only attracted to foods that work for me?" *or* "Why am I so motivated to workout?"

Make sure that you go through all five responses and get everyone to transfer all of their responses from the Subconscious Perspective to this page. You do not have to agonize over a question. All you have to do is keep asking and eventually the subconscious will come up with an answer.

CONSULTANT

Is anyone having a problem with turning any of your responses from the Subconscious Perspective into empowering questions? Let's move on to page 3 and **Step 3** of the program.

Step 3 - Subconscious Self-Image - Page 3

This is Step 3 of the program process which addresses the second component of MIND/ FITNESS which is your subconscious pictures.

1) Please describe in detail how you see yourself after you have attained your goals. (How you look and feel in mind, body, and spirit.)

Before we get started on this one, I would like to ask you a question: Do you feel good about yourself right now? Starting right now I want you to feel fantastic about yourself on all levels because once again it is like setting a goal. If you do not feel good about yourself right now, the mind has no place to go. This is one of your most important goals because it is in terms of the perception you have of yourself.

We have all heard of the term visualization but why is it important to visualize? It is important to visualize because it is like setting a goal, it gives your mind someplace to go. For example, if you see yourself as out of shape, insecure with your job or relationship or have a low self-image, the subconscious is going to do what ever it needs to do to keep you there.

How important is it that you establish the mental image of the person you would like to be? It is imperative. It is also important to check the image you have of yourself from time to time to make sure you are maintaining your new self-image. With this in mind

A) Do you see yourself firm and tone?

B) What is the weight of your new body?

C) What are the measurements of your chest, waist and hips?

D) How are other people reacting to you in this picture?

Statement 2

2) Please describe the activities you see yourself participating in after attaining your goals.

Questions for statement 2

A) Do you see yourself doing aerobics, jogging, lifting weights, going for a brisk walk, or maybe just parking further away from the entrance while going shopping?
On to statement 3

Statement 3

3) Please write down the feelings you experience from your new self image.

Questions for statement 3

A) Do you feel like you have become more of a magnet for everything you desire?

B) Do you feel a greater sense of spiritual strength?

C) What location could you put yourself in that would give you the most incredible feeling? Example: On vacation with someone you love, with family and friends or maybe in a quiet place just meditating.

D) Do you feel a tremendous sense of accomplishment? Not just over yourself but the things around you as well?

Let's go over what you have just written down. I will start with your first response.

Statement 1

1) Please describe in detail how you see yourself after you have attained your goals.

The most important image you will ever change is the image you have of yourself right now. It is essential that the image you have of yourself in your subconscious mind matches your goal. If it does not, the subconscious will do whatever it needs to, to maintain this image.

Writing down a detailed description of your new self-image will be the most effective way of implanting your new self-image into your subconscious. Going back and reading the description of your new self-image as part of your daily MIND/FITNESS program will make this image a permanent part of your new subconscious programming.

On to statement 2

Statement 2

2) Please describe the activities you see yourself participating in after attaining your goals.

It is imperative that you learn to associate activities that you know you will enjoy with your new self-image because becoming more active is an essential factor in attaining and maintaining a positive self-image.

On to statement 3

Statement 3

3) Please write down the feelings you experience from your new self image.

The subconscious will always move toward pleasure and away from pain. This is why it is crucial that your new subconscious self-image is detailed, crystal clear, and you derive tremendous pleasure from it.

You are now the writer, producer and director of your subconscious self-image. You can create the exact image you wish. You can participate in an activity you enjoy and in an emotional state and location that makes you feel incredible. Make your new subconscious body image as real and pleasurable as possible.

What do you do if you have a difficult time maintaining the new image? Questions play an important role here as well. If you are having a difficult time maintaining the new perception of yourself, you can ask questions like:

A) How can I maintain the image of this positive perception every second, every minute, every hour of the day?

B) What do I need to do to maintain this new image?

C) What can I add to this picture that might help me maintain this new image?

D) What do I need to do to feel fantastic all
the time?

E) What action do I need to take today that
will make me feel great?

Any time you run out of questions, what
question do you ask yourself?

A) What questions can I ask myself that will
help me maintain this new positive
empowering image?

There is one more variable here and that is
there might be something in the way of the
consistent maintenance of your new pictures.
A couple more questions might be:

A) What is getting in the way of the
maintenance of my new picture?
or

B) What do I need to unlearn that will clear
up the image of my new picture?

Are you with me? Are there any questions?
You need to go back and re-read your three
responses from the beginning every day
because you need to have a very clear vision
of how the new self appears and most
importantly how you feel in mind, body and
sprit.

Remember that every time you go back
and re-read this you are making an assault on

the old programming, and it is important to continue this assault until the subconscious accepts this new picture as how you should look and feel. Now let's take a look at the structure of your subconscious pictures.

The way you are able to determine positive from negative experiences is the way an image is stored or the structure of that image. Following, you will discover how you store the visual information that creates a positive emotional state for you; then, use that information to help you maintain your focus and motivation toward your goals.

I think we can all agree that we are all basically wired the same, but there is a reason one person loses motivation and another never quits. This lies in the way each of us codes our internal pictures. In other words, every person's perception of what they are doing is different. This is why two people can experience the same event but have a totally different perception or feeling about it.

Before we begin, you need to clearly understand how to associate and dissociate. Right now association and dissociation happens automatically; in other words, how you feel about events in your life and yourself determine whether you associate or dissociate with the experience. If you are out of shape, over or under eat, or are abusive toward your body, you are dissociating form it. Association and dissociation must be intentional if you want a greater level of control over how you feel.

Association and dissociation is the equivalent of you watching your life's movie. If I ask you to dissociate from a picture, that means that you are in the theater looking at yourself in the picture.

You may need to further dissociate from the picture if it is one that you are particularly uncomfortable with. This will mean that you will put yourself in the balcony looking down at yourself watching yourself in the picture. When I ask you to associate with a picture of yourself, this simply means that you place yourself in the picture and fully become part of that experience.

You will now begin with defining the structure of a subconscious picture. Think about your new self-image as you detailed it on this page and establish all the positive associated feelings of love, health, and wealth. Do whatever you need to fully focus and concentrate on the formation of this picture. When you look at this picture, you feel total love and feel life could not be better. It could be a vacation, a new love, or whatever you wish. You will refer to this picture as your motivation picture. Once you have established your new image, we will explore the composition.

Note:

This is a good time to ask someone if they would like to volunteer and describe the structure of their replacement picture.

CONSULTANT

Is the picture you see of that experience in color or black and white? If it is in black and white, turn it in to color. If it is already in color, make the colors more pleasing and vibrant. Is the picture framed, unframed, or panoramic? If the picture is framed or a certain size, make it panoramic so that it completely encompasses your field of vision. Is the picture moving like a film or is it still? If the picture is still, add movement. If the picture is too fast or too slow, adjust the speed so that it is completely comfortable for you.

Is there sound in the form of voices, music, ambient or nothing? If there is a voice or voices you find immensely pleasing, add them in and delete the rest. Now add your favorite music or ambient sound like ocean waves, birds chirping, or a gentle breeze.

Is the picture bright and clear or slightly out of focus? If the picture is out of focus, make it perfectly clear. If it is clear, make it brighter, sharper, and clearer until it is overwhelmingly pleasing. Take a few moments to structure this picture so that it is the most compelling experience you have ever had. Now associate with this picture and place yourself in this experience. Give yourself a moment to solidly plant yourself in this picture. Did you feel different when you became part of this experience?

Step out of this picture and put the image aside for a moment, and we will establish what you will refer to as your **GOAL PICTURE**. This time I want you to create a picture of yourself in a fitness program that you feel will establish the goal you have in mind for your mind, body, and sprit. Take a moment and be sure to get a clear image of this picture. When you have established the image, let's take a look at the composition.

Note:

Once again ask for a volunteer who is willing to describe their picture. Wait until they fully describe each component before moving on to the next one.

CONSULTANT

Is the picture in color or black and White? Is the picture framed, unframed, or panoramic? How big is the image and where is it located? Is the picture moving like a film or is it still?

If it is moving, is the speed fast, slow, or normal? Is there sound in the form, voices, ambient, or nothing? Is the picture bright and clear or slightly out of focus?

Once you have established the composition of the goal picture, I want you to bring back the motivation picture and place it in front of the goal picture. Step into the motivation picture and completely associate with the motivation picture. Now punch a tiny, tiny pinhole through the motivation picture so you can look through it and see the goal picture.

While looking through the pin-hole, begin to change the structure of the goal picture to match the motivation picture. In other words, if the goal picture is in black and white, turn it into color. Now make it panoramic. Do the same with the sound, speed, and resolution as well as any other differences you can see.

Once you have reframed your goal picture, change the image of yourself until you see exactly what you want. Pause for a moment to make sure the mind, body and spirit of the person in this picture is exactly what you want. Be sure to establish the exact physical dimensions you want, along with the purest feelings of love for the person in that picture.

Be sure you remain in the motivation picture while occasionally looking through the pinhole and seeing yourself totally in control and doing what you feel is completely necessary to accomplish your goals. If you have trouble restructuring the **Goal Picture** to match the motivation picture, you can fuse the goal picture with the **Motivation Picture**. In other words, move the goal picture into the motivation until both pictures become one and you see yourself in the motivation picture going through your daily fitness plan. This technique can be used with any objective in your life that needs a little more motivation behind it.

Now step out of the picture, put it aside for a moment, and we will move on to **Section 2** the Stop and Replace Samples.

Stop and Replace Samples

Like I said at the beginning of the program, these are samples of The Stop and Replace System and what you will be unlearning through the course of The Full Spectrum Program. You can refer back to these sheets and use this information to get started but only if you can identify and relate to the example. Let's move on to **Section 3** of the notebook and **Step 4** of the program, **The Stop and Replace System**.

Step 4 - The Stop and Replace System

The Stop and Replace System uses what you have learned in the first three pages of the program to **Recognize**, **Access** and **Change** the contents of your subconscious programming that does not work for you. This sheet will allow you to make dramatic changes in your emotional state and behavior by allowing you to change the contents of a subconscious program.

What are the key components of a subconscious program? Two key elements must exist in order to activate an emotional state, which in turn determines your behavior.

1) You must talk to yourself, which usually begins with a question

   and

2) By asking yourself a question, your subconscious mind will always give you an answer which in turn produces a correlating picture.

It is from this subconscious picture that your emotional state is determined and in turn determines your behavior. If you have a means of intervening on these two key components, you can make a change in the way you feel, which in turn changes your behavior.

The Stop and Replace System is where you make a full assault on the subconscious programs that do not work for you. Today we will be working on the three biggest ones, which are **Fear, Guilt** and **Anger** unless you decide on something else. The reason we start the program with these three emotions is that fear and guilt are used on all of us as children to try and control our behavior and at some point, fear and guilt turn into anger. These are also the three most limiting emotional states and the motivation behind a wide spectrum of behaviors that do not work. Some people think they have to have fear so they don't do things like jump off a tall building.

You do not have to be afraid of heights to keep yourself from jumping off a tall building. All you need to know is what the results will be.

Fear

At the top of the page, please write **Fear** in the first box with the arrow in it. If there is something specific to you such as fear of crowds, etc., write that in next to it. Fear can also include doubt, insecurity, etc. In other words you could be insecure about accomplishing your goals, about the way you look, about your relationships. All of these pertain to Fear.

Reasons for **NOT** doing this and Empowering Questions

In the left column below fear it states Reasons for **NOT** doing this. If you have a difficult time thinking of Reasons for not being fearful, refer to the **Stop and Replace** Samples. If you refer to the samples, only use the information there if it is specific to you. Remember, we also refer to the reasons for doing something as anchors so what you are doing is developing better reasons for not doing what you wish to unlearn. What might the advantages be for not being fearful? Can fear keep you from getting things done? Yes. If this applies write in: I will not procrastinate over things I know need to be done. In the right hand column, you will write a correlating Empowering Question. If you're positive anchor was, I will not procrastinate the **Empowering Question** would be, How can I unlearn procrastination? What you have now done is anchor yourself away from fear and asked a question that will begin to produce different results.

Something else has also happened here. We have also uncovered something else you want to unlearn, which is, of course, procrastination. Much of the time when you are writing down positive anchors, you will uncover other things that you may want to unlearn so always scrutinize your positive anchors for anything else you wish to unlearn.

What other positive anchors might there be for not being fearful? If you do not procrastinate you will be more productive so your next anchor might be: I will be more productive. The **Empowering Question** would then be: How can I increase my productivity? If you are not spending time on fear or procrastinating, then you would have a lot more time to spend on your food and fitness plan and other things you enjoy. So the next reason for not being fearful might be: I will have more time to spend on my food and fitness plan and other things I enjoy.

The **Empowering Question** would be: How can I find more time to spend on my food and fitness plan and other things I enjoy? Would the elimination of fear give you more control? Yes! So the last reason for not being fearful might be: I will have a greater sense of control over my environment and myself. The **Empowering Question** would be: How can I gain a greater level of control over my environment and myself?

Answers to Empowering Questions

Right below the anchors and **Empowering Question** you will see a space for Answers to **Empowering Questions**. Be sure to fill this in when the answers come to you. Remember you do not have to sit and work on a question. Just keep asking and the mind will eventually give you one. It is important to come back to this every day and continue asking these questions until you are completely happy with the answers.

Describe your Replacement Picture - Associated

Describe your Replacement Picture. The most important question to ask yourself when unlearning a behavior is: What can I use to replace this habit, behavior or emotional state that will benefit me? You cannot just quit something and leave a blank spot in the mind; you must replace it with something that you derive tremendous pleasure from before you quit. A good example of this is someone who says: I can't quit smoking, I'll gain weight. You gain weight because you did not make a conscious choice of what you were going to replace the habit with so the mind made a choice for you.

There are no limits for this replacement picture. You do, however, want to make the replacement picture as compelling as possible which means that you want to focus on the results as opposed to the process. In other words, everyone likes the results of exercise but very few people enjoy the process so it is important to create an image that is the most compelling to you.

The basis for this new picture needs to be a combination of the **results** of the goals you listed on the first page of the program and the description of the new self you wrote down on page three of the program. After establishing the picture of the new self, enhance it in any way that you possibly can. For instance, add music to it if you have a favorite song, add whatever colors you want or put people in the picture who make you feel good. Also, make sure that you always focus

on the results of your replacement picture.
For example: If fear is preventing you from
getting something done, you want to establish
a picture of having the task done of whatever
you were procrastinating over as opposed to
going through the process.

Describe your Old Picture - Dissociated

Now write down a description of the old
picture and remember to stay **dissociated** from
this picture. Do you remember how to
dissociate from your negative pictures?

Your Cue for Fear

After you've written down what the old picture
looks like, I want you to take a look at that
picture and then back it up until right before
you begin the behavior. This is known as your
cue.

The cue is the most difficult part of the
Stop and Replace System sheet so if you can
not think of the cue right now do not concern
yourself with it; just ask yourself the question:
What is the cue for this issue? It is important
to recognize the cue; so as soon as you think
of it, write it down.

The Switch Pattern for Fear

Now for the fun part, are you ready? We are going to learn how to do the **switch pattern**. First, I would like you to get a good clear vision of your Replacement Picture, Associated. Do you have a clear vision of your new picture? Once you have established that picture, set it aside for a moment.

Now bring up your Old Picture, Dissociated. Remember anytime we talk about the old picture, make sure you remain dissociated from it by putting yourself in the back row of a theatre as opposed to actually being part of the picture.

When you recognize the Cue in the old picture say "**STOP**" to yourself and then move the picture closer to you, make it smaller, smaller, darker and darker until it's a little black BB right in front of your face. Now shoot it back behind you and blow it up into a million molecules while saying "**REPLACE**" to yourself which will simultaneously bring up the new picture. That is the switch pattern. This is how you make a full assault on a behavior that does not work for you and create a positive permanent change in the subconscious. Are there any questions so far?

End Session One

Note:

If you are working within a time constraint, this is where you would stop the program and issue the following homework. If you are doing the entire program, drop down to where it says **Continued**.

CONSULTANT

This is where we end the program for today. Your homework between now and the next time I see you will be the following: start with page one of the first tab. You will find as time goes by that you will want to refine or completely change your goals, so **read over your goals every day.**

Next go to page 2 and reread all of your empowering questions before you go to bed at night and as soon as you get up each morning until you have answers for all of them.

After all of your questions are answered ask yourself: Am I satisfied with all the answers to my empowering questions? If the answer is no, you simply restructure the question until you are completely satisfied. **On to page three**

Reread this page every day to insure that you maintain your new self-image. If you have problems maintaining this new self image, then what questions do you ask yourself? Answer: What do I need to unlearn that is getting in the way of maintaining my new self image? **On to Section 3**

Section 3

I want you to reread the stop and replace system sheet until you are completely satisfied with the results. If you are not satisfied with the results by the next time I see you, we may need to restructure this sheet. If you feel you would like to work on more habits using the Stop and Replace System feel free to do so. **On to Section 4**

Section 4

I want you to ask yourself the five key questions every day. Those are...

1) Does this work for me?
2) How do I feel and will I benefit from the results of this? (If the answer to this question is no, ask yourself this next question).
3) What can I replace this with that I will benefit from?

The two key questions to use instead of reprimanding yourself are...

4) What can I learn from this?
   and
5) How can I use this experience to move myself more quickly toward my goals?

I also want you to ask at least two questions per category every day. Are there any questions?

DAY 2

Note:

If you split the program, this is where you pick it up.

CONSULTANT

How do you feel today? Please open your notebook to the first tab, and let's take a look at page 1. Are all of your goals still the same or do you need to make any changes?

Page 2 - Empowering Questions

Were you able to answer all of your empowering questions? If not, have you been asking yourself the questions every day? It is an **Absolute Must** that you ask yourself these questions every day until all the questions have been answered.

The next question is: Are you satisfied with your answers?

Note:

If someone is not satisfied with their answer, you need to help them restructure the question and continue to do so until they are completely satisfied with the answer. To get the answer you want, you need to have the right question. This is the key to making this program work.

CONSULTANT

If you are ever dissatisfied with an answer you must continue to restructure the question until you get the exact results you want. For example, if one of your goals was to lose 10 pounds and your empowering question was: How can I lose 10 pounds? The structure of this question may not produce an answer that is compelling to you, so you may need to restructure the question until you are completely satisfied with the results. What is compelling to you that you could add to this question?

Let's go to page 3, Subconscious Self-Image. Have you been able to maintain your new self-image, and if not, what do you need to do to maintain this image? You will want to address each statement on this page and make sure that MIND/FITNESS techniques are established to perpetuate the new self-image.

Let's go to The Stop and Replace System. Are you satisfied with the results of unlearning **Fear**?

Note:

If someone is not satisfied with the results of this page, ask them if they reread the page every day.

If they did and still did not get the results they wanted, you will need to start this page over with new reasons, empowering questions, a new replacement picture and a more definitive cue. Look for underlying issues that may need to be addressed in conjunction with fear.

Continued
CONSULTANT

Guilt

> Let's go to the next page. At the top of the page, write in Guilt unless there is something you feel is of greater importance to unlearn. If there is something specific to you such as food, exercise, procrastination etc, write that in next to it. For example: guilt from overeating, guilt from not exercising or guilt from procrastinating.

Reasons for NOT doing this and Empowering Questions

> In the left column below guilt, it states Reasons for **NOT** doing this. What might the advantages be for not being guilty? If you have a difficult time thinking of advantages for not being guilty, refer to The Stop and Replace samples. Remember, when you refer to a sample, only use the information there if it is specific to you. Now what might a big advantage be for unlearning guilt? What does guilt do to you? Guilt tends to help generate your negative self-talk.
> Unlearning guilt will help you eliminate

your negative self-talk. The reason or anchor then for not being guilty would be: "I will be able to eliminate my negative self-talk." If this is relative to you, write it down. An empowering question for this reason might be: "What do I need to do to permanently eliminate my negative self-talk?" You have also once again uncovered something you want to unlearn if you marked in eliminating **negative self talk** as one of your reasons or anchors.

What other reasons or anchors are there for not being guilty? If you unlearn guilt, will you feel better emotionally? Yes. So another reason for not being guilty is: "I will feel better emotionally." A suggestion for the correlating **Empowering Question** would then be: "What action do I need to take to improve my emotional state every day?" Does anyone have a reason or positive anchor they would like to volunteer?

Another reason for not feeling guilt is: "I will eliminate behaviors that make me feel guilty." The **Empowering Question** would be: "How can I permanently Stop behaviors that make me feel guilty."

Another reason for not being guilty is: "I will be able to eliminate guilt as an excuse for over eating, not exercising, etc. The **Empowering Question** would be: "How can I permanently eliminate guilt as an excuse for over or under eating and skipping my fitness plan?"

If you are done with Reasons for not doing this and Empowering Questions, let's move down to answers to **Empowering Questions**.

Answers to Empowering Questions

Be sure to fill in your Answers to **Empowering Questions** when the answers come to you. Let's drop down to your replacement picture.

Describe your Replacement Picture - Associated

Once again the basis for this new picture needs to be a combination of the **results** of the goals you listed on the first page of the program and the description of the new self you wrote down on page three of the program.

After establishing the picture of the new self, make sure the structure is the same as your initial replacement picture and enhance it in any way that you possibly can. For instance, add music to it if you have a favorite song, add whatever colors you want or put people in the picture who make you feel good.

Also, make sure you always focus on the results of whatever your replacement picture is. Always go for the results of not feeling guilty and Associate with this picture.

Describe your Old Picture - Dissociated

Make sure you keep yourself out in the audience of the theatre when viewing this picture or up in the balcony looking down at yourself looking at this picture.

Your Cue for Guilt

When you are done describing the old picture, continue to look at it and then run it backwards until right before you begin the behavior. This is your cue.

The Switch Pattern for Guilt

Are you ready for the switch pattern? First get a good clear vision of the new picture and make sure you are a part of it. Once you have established that picture, I want you to move it aside for a moment. Now establish a **dissociated** vision of the old picture.

When you recognize the cue in the old picture say "**STOP**" to yourself and then move the picture closer to you, make it smaller, smaller, darker, and darker until it's a little black BB right in front of your face.

Now shoot it back behind you and blow it up into a million molecules while saying to yourself "**REPLACE**" which simultaneously brings up the new picture. Are there any questions for this page? **On to the next page.**

Anger

Is there anyone who has never experienced the emotion of anger? In the box at the top of the page please write in anger.

If there is something specific, add that in such as; if you have anger toward yourself, a family member, a friend, your boss or the way your life is going.

Reasons for NOT doing this and Empowering Questions

What might the positive anchors be for not being angry? What is usually significantly impaired when you get angry? Do you begin to communicate differently? Yes. So your first reason or positive anchor for not being angry might be: I will not lose control of my ability to communicate effectively. And of course the **Empowering Question** would be: How can I improve my communication skills?

What other benefits might there be for not being angry? Do you ever stuff this emotion with food? If your answer is yes, then your next reason for not doing this might be: I will not be able to use anger as an excuse to over or under eat. The **Empowering Question** would be: How can I eliminate anger as an excuse to over or under eat.

Would you be more loving toward

yourself, your family and others? Yes. If this pertains to you, please write it down. The **Empowering Question** for this reason would be: How can I be more loving toward my family, others and myself? Would you have more fun with life? Yes. If this pertains to you, another reason might be: I will have more fun with life. The **Empowering Question** would be: How can I have more fun with everything I do in life?

Answers to Empowering Questions

Be sure to fill this in your Answers to **Empowering Questions** when the answers come to you. Let's drop down to your replacement picture.

Describe your Replacement Picture - Associated

When you have finished the positive anchors and **Empowering Questions**, go to the bottom of the page and describe the new picture associated.

Once again, the basis for your new picture needs to be a combination of the **RESULTS** of the goals you listed on the first page of the program and the description of the new self you wrote down on page three of the program.

After establishing the picture of the new self, make sure the structure is the same as your initial replacement picture and enhance it in any way that you possibly can. For instance, add music to it if you have a favorite song, add whatever colors you want or put people in the picture who make you feel good. Also, make sure that you always focus on the results of your replacement picture.

Describe your Old Picture - Dissociated

When you have finished describing the new picture, describe the old picture, **dissociated**.

You're Cue for Anger

Do you have the new and the old picture written down? We're you able to recognize your cue? If you were not able to clearly recognize your cue, just ask your self the question: What is the cue for this picture?

The Switch Pattern for Anger

Are you ready for the switch pattern? First, get a clear vision of the new picture and make sure you are a part of it. Once you have established that picture, I want you to move it aside for a moment. Now establish a **dissociated** vision of the old picture.

When you recognize the cue in the old picture, say "**STOP**" to yourself and then move the picture closer to you, make it smaller, smaller, darker, and darker until it's a little black BB right in front of your face. Now shoot it back behind you and blow it up into a million molecules while saying "**REPLACE**" to yourself which simultaneously brings up the new picture.

Every time you reread your Stop and Replace sheet, you are making an assault on the old subconscious programming. This is why it is imperative that read every **STOP and REPLACE** sheet every day to make sure every habit, behavior, or emotion has been changed to your satisfaction.

If you have not begun to see significant results after 7 days, you will need to use another blank Stop and Replace sheet and rewrite all of your reasons, **Empowering Questions**, new and old picture, and of course, a clear identification of your cue. Are there any questions? On to **Section 4** of the notebook and **Step 5** of the program The Heart of MIND/FITNESS.

Step 5 - The Heart of MIND/FITNESS

Let's take a look at Tab Four. This is The Heart of MIND/FITNESS. The Heart of MIND/FITNESS consists of your **Love - Health - Wealth - Self Image.**

Once you understand how to take control of your emotional state, it is imperative that you use these skills on a daily basis. The way you process information can be dramatically changed in a short period of time, simply by consistently implementing The Heart of MIND/FITNESS. Feel free to bend, shape, rearrange and change any and all questions to suit your exact needs.

It is imperative that you ask yourself a minimum of one question per category every night before you go to bed and every morning after you get up. This is the least you must do in order to maintain your minimum MIND/ FITNESS.

The First Three Key Questions You Will Ask Yourself Through the Course of Your Day Are:

1) Does this work for me?
2) How do I feel and will I benefit from the results of this? (If the answer is no, ask yourself this next question).
3) What can I replace this with that will benefit me?

The Two Key Questions to Use Instead of Reprimanding Yourself Are...

4) What can I learn from this?
   and
5) How can I use this to move myself more quickly toward my goals?

The first of these five questions is the most important because you can plug a lot of different things into it, for instance: Does this program work for me? I want you to ask yourself this question because my objective is to insure your success and I have the resources to do that, but I need to know what is working and what does not.

Other things that you may want to plug into this first key question are: Does my food plan work for me? Does my fitness plan work for me? Does this relationship work for me?

The second question is important because there are things in your life that you think may work for you, but you may not benefit from the results. The best example of this is cigarette smokers.

If I ask a smoker: Does smoking work for you? The image they will usually see initially is kicking back, relaxing and enjoying their cigarette; so the initial answer is many times "yes." If I then ask them: How do you feel and will you benefit from the results of smoking? This brings up a totally different picture especially, if you ask them to look at the results 10, 20 or 30 years from now.

You now see someone whose mouth looks like a puckered rectum and breathing has become difficult. You have significantly shortened your life and the quality of your life.

The third question is important because

you can not leave a blank spot in the mind. If you do not make a choice for replacement of an emotion, habit or behavior, the mind will make one for you. The whole point of this program process is not to become who you are by accident, especially if it simply does not work.

Asking these last two questions allows you to use every experience in your life. Nothing in life is negative or useless if you know how to use it.

You also want to make sure that you continue to go back and reread all the **Empowering Questions** you have written down on page 2 of the program and continue to restructure them until you get an answer that is completely satisfactory to you.

Let's move on to Section 5 of the notebook and Step 6 of the program, your Food and Fitness Planner.

Step 6 - Food and Fitness Planner

Getting consistent control of your emotional state includes consistent control of what you eat, drink, and the type and amount of exercise. Why is it important to plan your food and fitness schedule? It is important because the process of a subconscious assault on the body with food, alcohol, or drugs can start a day or even days before you indulge in it. This will throw you completely off course and out of control. Planning your food and fitness schedule is a big part of reprogramming these unwanted behaviors. You need to plan them until it becomes automatic. Starting from the top, you have a start and end date and then the week is divided into every other day.

This is split up so that if you are just starting, it does not become overwhelming to try and plan a food and fitness schedule every day. You always want to plan your food and fitness schedule the day before so on this first page you start on Sunday and plan your food schedule for Monday. If you choose, you can plan your food schedule every other day and your fitness schedule every other day. If you are feeling enthusiastic, you can plan both your food and fitness plan every day prior to the day of implementation.

The instruction set for your food and fitness plan and emotionally driven food are at the bottom of each page. People who weigh themselves every day are more successful at maintaining a consistent weight. As long as this does not become another obsessive habit, it will help to maintain an association with your body. You must ultimately determine if this is going to work for you.

You have enough Food and Fitness Planner sheets for 30 days. You can of course make more copies if you need them.

Let's move on to **Step 7**, Maintenance and The Trance-Formation. This is the last step in the program process of MIND/FITNESS.

Step 7 - The Trance-Formation

The Trance-Formation is a MIND/FITNESS tool that you will use at least once a day for the rest of your life. What does the term Trance-Formation mean? The term Trance is used to describe a subconscious state, or what some people refer to as meditation or prayer. It is a means of having a greater level of communication with the subconscious. The last half of this term, Formation, refers to the formation of information during your Trance or the structure of your self-talk and pictures. The best time to change the structure of stored information is when you are as close as you can get to a subconscious state or trance.

Instead of being given generic information during your trance, the information used during this part of the program will be specific to you as established in the first six steps.

What you say to yourself is more important than anything anyone will ever say to you or about you. Once you have learned the dialogue of the induction, you can use this to put yourself in a relaxed state that will allow you greater control over your subconscious processes. The primary question before beginning this process is: What is my most powerful emotional state? Your most powerful emotional state is love, and this is the supreme goal when restructuring your subconscious programming. Please make yourself comfortable and we will begin.

Note:

This part of the program needs to be done by someone who is experienced at hypnotherapy. If you are not, simply use the CD from the book or from Programming Your Fit Mind. **The Trance** is the dialogue for the induction.

CONSULTANT

The Trance

First, establish a clear vision of your motivation picture and the new self as detailed in The Heart of MIND/FITNESS. When viewing this picture, make sure that your body is the exact dimensions you wish you are with people you love and in a location that makes you feel fantastic.

Once you have a clear vision of your motivation picture and your new self, please set it aside for a moment and you will begin the process of the Trance-Formation.

Start by placing your palms face up on your thighs. Now put two swirling white lights in the center of your palms. In your left palm, place your favorite animal or animals and in the right palm, place the old self dissociated. Take a look at your animal or animals in this light. What are they doing? Now take a look at the old self: What is the old self doing? Keep your eyes on the old self...now **FIRE** the old self and replace it with the new self in this swirling white light. Now take a deep breath in through your nose and slowly exhale through your mouth as you bring your palms up to your chest and this swirling warm white loving light enters your chest. Take another deep breath in through your nose and slowly exhale out through your mouth as your eyes become heavy and fall from their own weight.

With every breath, you become more and more relaxed as this warm white loving light moves through the entire cavity of the chest...illuminating every cell and any dark areas of the body. This white light continues to move up your neck and into your skull...illuminating every cell of the brain while moving back down into your neck, down your shoulders into your arms, and out to the end of your fingertips. This warm white light continues to move down into the cavity of your stomach as you begin to see a set of stairs, ten steps to the bottom.

As you take the first step down these stairs, you go down a thousand steps and become more relaxed as this warm white swirling light continues to move down into your legs, into your feet, and out through the ends of your toes. As you take the second third and forth steps, you continue to go down a thousand steps with each step, and this warm white light expands outward and completely encompasses you, illuminating every cell and destroying any dark areas of the consciousness and body. This warm, white loving light becomes focused and concentrated on any areas of the body that may need to be healed and remain there until the problem is dissolved and replaced by new healthy cells.

Looking upward you begin to see a clear image of your motivation picture. You see yourself and the structure of the picture just as you described it in The Subconscious Self Image. You are in a location that makes you feel incredible with all the people, colors, and sounds that you desire. This picture is panoramic and fully encompasses your field of vision. You step into this picture and become fully associated with it

As you begin to absorb all the good feelings of this picture, you punch a tiny, tiny pinhole in your motivation picture so that you can look through and see your goal picture. The picture you see of yourself is at the exact weight and fitness level you have chosen, and you are in a fitness program you enjoy. As you

look at your goal picture through the tiny
pinhole, make sure that the goal picture is the
same in composition as the motivation picture.
In other words make sure that it is panoramic,
in color, and with similar sounds as well as
any other differences you can see. Looking at
your goal picture, you begin to ask yourself
the first two key questions

1) Does this work for me?

2) How do I feel and will I benefit from the
results of this? (If the answer to this is no,
then you ask yourself the next key
question).

3) What can I use to replace this with that will
benefit me?

You continue to reshape and change what you
are doing and the contents of the picture until
you get exactly what you want. Nothing ever
stays the same and neither will the pictures in
your mind. You now step out of your
motivation picture and back onto the fourth
step.

With your motivation picture in clear view,
you continue going down the stairs to the fifth,
sixth and seventh steps. You continue to go
down a thousand steps with each step. This
warm, white loving light continues to swirl
within you and around you becoming the
perfect magnet for everything you desire.

As you view your motivation picture, other
pictures begin to emerge. These are pictures
of you going through your daily routine:

working, playing, and interacting with people and things. Some of these pictures may be of you skipping your fitness program or making a mistake and you begin to reprimand yourself. You immediately recognize this and begin to ask yourself the next two key questions.

4) What can I learn from this?

and

5) How can I use this experience to move myself more quickly toward my goals?

If an answer does not come right away, you continue to chant these questions until the mind is no longer capable of reprimanding.

Suddenly the power of these and other **Empowering Questions** begin to work for you, and you find that something that just seemed useless or even harmful now becomes useful and empowering.

This warm, white loving light continues to move through your body and expanding outward. Your Mind, Body, and Spirit become fully integrated. All of your goals and the ways to accomplish them begin to come in clear view.

As other pictures come into view, there are some that cannot be used. You immediately ask yourself: Does this image work for me? When the answer is no, you immediately say **Stop** to yourself.

This immediately initiates the switch pattern and makes the picture smaller, smaller, darker, darker until it is a little black BB in front of your face and shoot it back behind you and blow it up into a billion molecules. You then say **Replace** to yourself while simultaneously bringing up your motivation picture. You initiate this process a thousand times a second if that is what it takes to destroy the old picture. You fully understand that you are the one who now controls the subconscious.

You continue to relax with every breath you take, and you get all the good feelings of the motivation picture. Concentrating on this picture, you continue to relax, feeling good about both images and still going deeper and deeper, with every breath. While keeping your motivation picture in view, another warm, white loving light that you call upon any time you need to, enters through the top of your head moving down into the skull adding to the light that is already there.

Every night as you go to bed you call upon this loving light and begin to create your own dialogue that will allow you to enter a subconscious state. This warm, white light continues to enter the top of your skull, moving down into the neck, into shoulders, down your arms and out through the ends of your fingers illuminating every cell along the way.

As you continue to go deeper and deeper, this warm white light moves down into the chest, abdomen, and continues into the legs and feet.

This warm white light continues to pour down through the top of the head, filling every cell and then it expands, completely surrounding you. As you become empowered from this powerful white loving light, you continue down the stairs to the eighth, ninth, and tenth steps.

You now step back into the motivation picture, getting all the good feelings of this picture while occasionally looking through the pinhole and seeing your goal picture; allowing all the incredible feelings of the motivation picture to fill your entire body.

You continue to go deeper and deeper as questions begin to enter your mind. **Empowering Questions** that will maintain and perpetuate your, love, health, wealth, and self image. Questions for your emotional and spiritual **LOVE** begin to emerge.

-What do I need to do to keep my love from turning into fear, guilt or anger?

-How can I continually and perpetually live in this of light of love?

-How can I be more of a magnet for loving energy?

-What action do I need to take to realize the full potential of my emotional and spiritual love?

-How can I use my emotional and spiritual love to improve my communication skills?

-What do I need to do to perceive all past and current relationships as beneficial?

-What will happen today that will give me incredible pleasure for no reason?

-What questions do I need to ask myself to perpetuate a healthy emotional and spiritual love?

As this warm, white loving light continues to pour down through the top of your head and destroys any dark areas while illuminating every cell. **Empowering Questions** for your **Health** begin to emerge while your subconscious continues to work on the questions for your love:

-What action do I need to take to maintain a consistent fitness program?

-What do I need to do to feel this good all the time?

-How can I make sure I stay in the habit of changing things that do not work for me?

-How can I maintain my excitement and enthusiasm over my fitness program every day?

-What exercise do I enjoy enough to make a permanent part of my daily or weekly routine?

-How can I make sure I only ask questions that work for me and move me quickly toward my goals?

-What emotional state do I need to change that may be keeping me from my optimum health?

-How can I make sure that mind, body and spirit are always fully integrated?

-What other questions do I need to ask that will keep me moving toward and perpetuate my desired health?

As your subconscious continues to work on the questions for your Love and Health, your **Wealth** questions begin to emerge.

-What action do I need to take to initiate and perpetuate my desired wealth?

-What action do I need to take to maximize my productivity every day?

-What do I need to do to perceive every experience as a positive?

-What do I need to do to become more of a magnet for everything I desire?

-How can I make all things in life work for me?

-How can I increase my decision-making speed?

-What other questions do I need to ask that will keep me moving toward my desired wealth?

As your love, health and wealth questions continue, your **Self-Image** questions begin to emerge.

-How can I maintain the image of this positive perception every second, every minute, every hour of the day?

-What do I need to do to maintain my motivation picture and the image of the new self?

-What can I add to the picture that will help me maintain this new image?

-What do I need to do to feel fantastic all the time?

-What action do I need to take today that will make me feel great?

-What information do I need to perpetuate my love, health, wealth and self-image?

-What questions do I need to ask myself every day that will insure my emotional well-being?

-What information do I need to insure the success of my goals?

As you continue to ask yourself **Empowering Questions,** the warm white light begins to swirl at your feet as you begin to go back up the stairs to the ninth, eighth, seventh, and sixth steps. With every breath, you pull this energy up into your legs, abdomen, chest, arms, hands, neck and head as you continue to walk back up the stairs to the fifth, fourth, third, and second steps. As you step up to the first step and then the top of the stairs, your motivation picture becomes clearer than ever.

Your body now becomes completely and fully energized and as soon as you wish you may open your eyes.

You now know what your mind is doing next time you suffer from a lack of motivation. You can place your motivation picture in front of any goal picture that you feel is not moving fast enough or if there is an image that is not working for you, change the picture and the questions.

Be ye Transformed by the Renewing of Your Mind

CONSULTANT

Maintaining Your Fit Mind

The only way you can get consistent results with anything is to act consistently. In other words now that you have the tools to **Recognize**, **Access** and **Change** your subconscious programming, it is up to you to consistently implement these tools until you are completely satisfied that you have reprogrammed yourself. Page 1 of The Subconscious Perspective is a good page to return to if you're losing focus on your goals. It will always remind you of why you **Absolutely Must** accomplish your goals.

If you were unable to notice a difference when trying to unlearn something, there are a couple of things you can do.

1) Read over your **Stop and Replace** sheets every day.

2) If you do not recognize some change within 48 hours, move it to another day and mark in new anchors, new questions, and refine your replacement picture.

3) If you still do not notice a difference, scrutinize your **Reasons for NOT doing this** for underlying issues that you may need to unlearn.

What is the one behavior that would keep this program or any other program from working? The answer is lying. If you have a tendency to lie, then what does that allow you to do? It allows you to maintain a state of denial because if you are in the habit of lying, who is the person you will lie to the most often? **You** are the person you will lie to most often. If you recognize that you are not telling the truth most of the time, then you need to go back to the Stop and Replace System and address that as a behavior you need to unlearn. This behavior is of course rooted in the emotional state of fear.

The purpose of the Burris MIND/FITNESS Full Spectrum Program is to help you establish a solid foundation by which you can intervene in your behavior.

You absolutely must continue to use the principles of this program everyday if you expect and want to have control over your emotional state and your behavior.

One question always asked is: "Will a behavior that I have unlearned come back?" It is most certainly possible that a behavior will return, but this time you have the tools you need to repeat positive results.

If a behavior or an emotion that does not work for you comes back, just ask yourself a question: How was I able to make a positive change with this emotion or behavior before, and then repeat those actions?

It is also important to remember to turn your excuses into empowering questions as soon as they arise. Repeat them as questions everyday until you have pulled that anchor.

You may not be able to change what has happened to you, what is happening to you, or what is going to happen to you, but now you can change your perception of it. Make sure every life experience works for you instead of against you. Are there any questions?

Thank you for your participation in The **Burris MIND/FITNESS Full Spectrum Program.** The most advanced system for communication and behavior change.

Follow Up

Note:

It is imperative that you follow-up with your clients once a week for 30 days. This will make sure the processes of unlearning that was established through the course of the program remain in tact. If you call a client or meet with them, always start out at the beginning of the program and ask the following questions.

Subconscious Perspective - Page 1

CONSULTANT

Are you happy with the progression of your goals?

Empowering Questions - Page 2

Are you happy with all of the answers to all of your **Empowering Questions**?

Note:

If the answer to this last question is "no" or "I do not know", ask the client to volunteer a question that you can help them restructure. If they or you cannot think of a question, ask yourself this: What questions can I think of that will resolve this issue?

CONSULTANT

Subconscious Self-Image - Page 3

Have you been able to maintain your new self-image?

Note:

The answer to this will almost always be "no" or "not really". If this is the case, then this is definitely something you will want to work on in the **STOP and Replace System**.

Note:

The issue at the top of the Stop and Replace System would be, "Not Maintaining My New Self Image." You may also want to replace this page and have the client rewrite their responses.

The Stop and Replace System

Note:

Start from the first thing that your client worked on and continue until you reach a blank page, Ask the following questions per each completed page of the Stop and Replace System.

CONSULTANT

Are you completely happy with the results of this issue?

Note:

If the answer to this is "no" or "I do not know", then ask the following question: Would you like to address this issue again? If the answer to this is yes, then you need to help them fill out another Stop and Replace System sheet with all new information and continue the assault.

CONSULTANT

Have you been reading this page every day?

Note:

If the answer to this is "No," then you must insist that in order for them to reprogram themselves that they must read this every day. If they have been reading it every day, then you need to start a new page with this same issue.

CONSULTANT

Has anything else come up that you would like
to unlearn?

The Heart of MIND/FITNESS

Have you picked out a minimum of 4 questions
and are you reading those questions out loud
to yourself everyday?

Food & Fitness Plan

Have there been any foods that were
emotionally driven?

Note:

If the answer to this is "Yes," then ask them to identify the emotion
and then move it to the Stop and Replace System.

If you are on the phone, ask the following question: Would you
like to come in for another consultation? Your approach to follow up
consultations will depend on how these questions are answered. Do
not be afraid to do some handholding and step your client or patient
through the same issues if they are not achieving the results they
desire. Your clients and patients need a support system, and this may
consist of just you for now but try to help them establish one by
offering discounted rates for groups.

There are seven more Stop and Replace samples to use for follow
up consultations. You also may have to go back and address issues
that you worked on initially. Whatever the case, MIND/FITNESS is
the clearly defined process for empowering your clients or patients.

As time goes on, you will become more proficient and creative with your questions. This will allow you to make sure that the work you did in the first day is not diminished over the next 20 years.

What can you do to make sure all of your clients or patients continue to make a positive progression toward their goals?

Kelly Burris

APPENDIX B

BIBLIOGRAPHY

Chapter 3

[1] Clinical Guidelines on the Identification, Evaluation, and Treatment of Overweight and Obesity in Adults. National Institutes of Health, National Heart, Lung, and Blood Institute. June 1998.

[2] World Health Organization. Obesity: Preventing and managing the global epidemic. Report of a WHO Consultation on Obesity, Geneva, 3-5 June, 1997. World Health Organization. Geneva: 1998.

[3] Flegal KM, Carroll MD, Kuczmarski RJ, Johnson CL. Overweight and obesity in the United States: Prevalence and trends, 1960–1994. *International Journal of Obesity.* 1998;22:39–47.

[4] Kuczmarski RJ, Flegal KM. Criteria for definition of overweight in transition: Background and recommendations for the United States. *American Journal of Clinical Nutrition.* 2000;72:1074-1081.

[5] Physical status: The use and interpretation of anthropometry. Report of a WHO Expert Committee. World Health Organization: Geneva, 1995 (WHO Technical Report Series; 854).

[6] International Obesity Task Force. Managing the global epidemic of obesity. Report of the WHO Consultation on Obesity, Geneva, June 5–7, 1997. World Health Organization: Geneva.

[7] U.S. Department of Health and Human Services. The Surgeon General's Call to Action to Prevent and Decrease Overweight and Obesity, 2001.

[8] Flegal KM, Carroll MD, Ogden CL, Johnson CL. Prevalence and trends in obesity among US adults, 1999-2000. *Journal of the American Medical Association.* 2002;288:1723-1727.

[9] Pastor PN, Makuc DM, Reuben C, Xia H. Chartbook on Trends in the Health of Americans. Health, United States, 2002. Hyattsville, MD: National Center for Health Statistics. 2002.

[10] Mokdad AH, Ford ES, Bowman BA, Dietz WH, Vinicor F, Bales VS, Marks JS. Prevalence of obesity, diabetes, and obesity-related health risk factors, 2001. *Journal of the American Medical Association.* 2003;289(1):76-79.

[11] Mokdad AH, Bowman BA, Ford ES, Vinicor F, Marks JS, Koplan JP. The continuing epidemics of obesity and diabetes in the United States. *Journal of the American Medical Association.* 2001;286(10):1195-1200.

[12] Ogden CL, Flegal KM, Carroll MD, Johnson CL. Prevalence and trends in overweight among US children and adolescents, 1999-2000. *Journal of the American Medical Association.* 2002;288:1728-1732.

[13] Kuczmarski RJ, Ogden CL, Guo SS, et al. 2000 CDC growth charts for the United States: Methods and development. National Center for Health Statistics. Vital Health Statistics 11(246). 2002.

[14] Personal communication from Maureen I. Harris, NIDDK/ NIH, to Susan Z. Yanovski, NIDDK/NIH, 1999.

[15] Centers for Disease Control and Prevention. National diabetes fact sheet: General information and national estimates on diabetes in the United States, 2000. Atlanta, GA: U.S. Department of Health and Human Services, Centers for Disease Control and Prevention, 2002.

[16] National Institute of Diabetes and Digestive and Kidney Diseases. Diabetes Prevention Program Meeting Summary. August 2001. Diabetes Mellitus Interagency Coordinating Committee

[17] Brown CD, Higgins M, Donato KA, Rohde RC, Garrison R, Obarzanek E, Ernst ND, Horan M. Body mass index and prevalence of hypertension and dyslipidemia. *Obesity Research.* 2000;8(9):605-619

[18] Calle EE, Rodriguez C, Walker-Thurmond K, Thun MJ. Overweight, obesity, and mortality from cancer in a prospectively studied cohort of U.S. adults. *New England Journal of Medicine.* 2003; 348(17):1625-1638.

[19] Ballard-Barbash R, Swanson CA. Body weight: Estimation of risk for breast and endometrial cancers. *American Journal of Clinical Nutrition.* 1996; 63(suppl):437S–441S.

[20] Huang Z, Hankinson SE, Colditz GA, et al. Dual effects of weight and weight gain on breast cancer risk. *Journal of the America Medical Association.* 1997;278:1407–1411.

[21] Clinical Guidelines on the Identification, Evaluation, and Treatment of Overweight and Obesity in Adults—The Evidence Report. National Institutes of Health. *Obesity Research.* 1998;6 (suppl)2:51S-209S.

[22] Fontaine KR, Redden DT, Wang C, Westfall AO, Allison DB. Years of life lost due to obesity. *Journal of the American Medical Association.* 2003; 289(2):187-93.

[23] Wolf, AM, Manson JE, Colditz GA. The Economic Impact of Overweight, Obesity and Weight Loss. In: Eckel R, ed. *Obesity: Mechanisms and Clinical Management.* Lippincott, Williams and Wilkins; 2002.

[24] Wolf AM, Colditz GA. Current estimates of the economic cost of obesity in the United States. *Obesity Research.* March 1998; 6(2):97–106.

[25] Finkelstein EA, Fiebelkorn IC, Wang G. National medical spending attributable to overweight and obesity: How much, and who's paying? *Health Affairs Web Exclusive.* 2003;W3:219-226. Available at www.healthaffairs.org/WebExclusives/ Finkelstein_Web_Excl_051403.htm.

[26] Colditz GA. Economic costs of obesity. *American Journal of Clinical Nutrition.* 1992;55:503-507s.

[27] Barnes MA, Schoenborn CA. Physical activity among adults: United States, 2000. National Center for Health Statistics. *Advance Data.* 2003;(333).

[28] U.S. Department of Health and Humans Services. Physical Activity and Health: A Report of the Surgeon General. Centers for Disease Control and Prevention. 1996.

[29] Colditz GA. Economic costs of obesity and inactivity. *Medicine & Science in Sports & Exercise.* 1999; S663-S667.

Chapter 4

[1]American Psychiatric Association Work Group on Eating Disorders. Practice guideline for the treatment of patients with eating disorders (revision). *American Journal of Psychiatry*, 2000; 157(1 Suppl): 1-39

Links to resources for this chapter

National Institute of Mental Health (NIMH)
www.nimh.nih.gov

Harvard Eating Disorders Center
www.hedc.org

National Association of Anorexia Nervosa and Associated Disorders
www.anad.org
National Eating Disorders Association
www.nationaleatingdisorders.org

Academy for Eating Disorders
www.aedweb.org

National Foundation for Depressive Illness, Inc
www.depression.org

National Association of Cognitive-Behavioral Therapists'
www.NABCT.org

INDEX

Why is it broken? 10, 14
why you eat 19
Withdrawal 48
women 5, 34, 36, 38, 45, 50, 190,
     201
Women's Program. 5
Workdays lost 40
workout 3, 162, 214
writer 109

Y

yoga class 212
your eating behavior programming
     19
your emotional state 14, 16, 18, 25,
     58, 60, 115, 153, 177, 216